T0312310

Cambridge Elements ≡

Elements in the Philosophy of Biology
edited by
Grant Ramsey
KU Leuven
Michael Ruse
Florida State University

ANIMAL MODELS OF HUMAN DISEASE

Sara Green
University of Copenhagen

CAMBRIDGE
UNIVERSITY PRESS

Shaftesbury Road, Cambridge CB2 8EA, United Kingdom

One Liberty Plaza, 20th Floor, New York, NY 10006, USA

477 Williamstown Road, Port Melbourne, VIC 3207, Australia

314–321, 3rd Floor, Plot 3, Splendor Forum, Jasola District Centre, New Delhi – 110025, India

103 Penang Road, #05–06/07, Visioncrest Commercial, Singapore 238467

Cambridge University Press is part of Cambridge University Press & Assessment, a department of the University of Cambridge.

We share the University's mission to contribute to society through the pursuit of education, learning and research at the highest international levels of excellence.

www.cambridge.org
Information on this title: www.cambridge.org/9781009507318

DOI: 10.1017/9781009025836

First published 2024

A catalogue record for this publication is available from the British Library.

ISBN 978-1-009-50731-8 Hardback
ISBN 978-1-009-01230-0 Paperback
ISSN 2515-1126 (online)
ISSN 2515-1118 (print)

Animal Models of Human Disease

Elements in the Philosophy of Biology

DOI: 10.1017/9781009025836
First published online: March 2024

Sara Green
University of Copenhagen
Author for correspondence: Sara Green, sara.green@ind.ku.dk

Abstract: The crucial role of animal models in biomedical research calls for philosophical investigation of how and whether knowledge about human diseases can be gained by studying other species. This Element delves into the selection and construction of animal models to serve as preclinical substitutes for human patients. It explores the multifaceted roles animal models fulfil in translational research and how the boundaries between humans and animals are negotiated in this process. The Element also covers persistent translational challenges that have sparked debates across scientific, philosophical, and public arenas regarding the limitations and future of animal models. Among them are persistent tensions between standardization and variation in medicine, as well as between strategies aiming to reduce and recapitulate biological complexity. Finally, the Element examines the prospects of replacing animal models with animal-free methods. The Element demonstrates why animal modeling should be of interest to philosophers, social scientists, and scientists alike.

Keywords: animal models, animal-based research, translational models, preclinical research, animal-free methods

ISBNs: 9781009507318 (HB), 9781009012300 (PB), 9781009025836 (OC)
ISSNs: 2515-1126 (online), 2515-1118 (print)

Contents

1 Introduction

Our dependence on other species in biomedical research and medicine calls for philosophical scrutiny. Several hundred million animals are used worldwide each year in preclinical research and for drug testing, with mice and rats alone counting about 120 million animals (Taylor and Alvarez 2019; Carbone 2021; Cait et al. 2022).[1] Animal models serve as proxies for human diseases in a basic research and drug development, but the benefits and limitations of animal models are contested topics in science, bioethics, and public debates. How – and to what extent – can we learn about humans by studying and experimenting on animal models? What functions do animal models play in biomedical research, and why are specific animals chosen for specific purposes? How are boundaries between humans and animals constructed and negotiated in this process, socially and experimentally, and what are the main translational challenges and ethical concerns? And, given persistent problems of translational failures, what are the prospects of replacing animal models with animal-free methods in the future? This Element delves into these questions and highlights the intertwinement of epistemic, practical, and ethical issues faced in translational research. I hope this Cambridge Element will raise questions of interest to philosophers, social scientists, and scientists alike.

Another Cambridge Element on *Model Organisms* already covers many of the philosophical implications of the use of animal models in the life sciences (Ankeny and Leonelli 2020). Why this additional Element on *Animal Models of Human Disease*? This Element is focused on animal models used in the context of translational models, that is, on animal models that are *human-directed.* While many animal models in translational research are *model organisms* in the sense defined by Ankeny and Leonelli, the two terms should not be conflated. Model organisms are non-human organisms that are standardized to display general genetic or physiological features, and they thus have a broad representational scope and institutional support structure that allow for cross-species knowledge integration (Ankeny and Leonelli 2011; Leonelli and Ankeny 2012). Because model organisms are used to study general physiological features across a variety of species, their role as models cannot be reduced to the epistemic interest in improving human health. For example, the reliance on the thale cress, *Arabidopsis thaliana,* as a model organism in plant biology does not hinge on the relevance for human health (Leonelli 2007).[2]

---

[1] The numbers are estimated from registers of ethics approvals, including only animals that are *legally* considered to have moral status, i.e., it does not include most invertebrate species. See Sections 5 and 6 for further discussion.

[2] This, however, does not leave out the possibility that studies on *Arabidopsis thaliana* can inform human genomics and medicine (e.g., Jones et al. 2008).

Thus, the focus of this Element is in this sense narrower in zooming in on how and why animals, or parts of animals, are used for the specific purpose of learning about human diseases or improving human health (Huber and Keuck 2013).[3] But the focus is also broader in the sense that not all human-directed models are subsets of model organisms. As illustrated in this Element, translational animal models take on a variety of epistemic roles that are worth exploring as separate topics.

Animal models of human disease do not necessarily represent a large class of organisms, or even a large group of humans. They may, for example, serve as *surrogate models* that "stand in" for specific patient groups or even specific patients in drug development or drug testing (Bolker 2009; Green et al. 2021). Some animal models are also investigated as what some scientists call *negative models* because their resistance to human diseases or pathological conditions is medically relevant (Green et al. 2018). Moreover, animals can play more *instrumental roles* in medicine as diagnostic tools or detection devices that are not easily accounted for through a standard account of scientific models as representations of targets (Germain 2014; Knuuttila 2021). Scrutinizing the various functions of animals in biomedical research can therefore extend and deepen philosophical discussions on modeling in general. Translational research can also offer insights into the epistemic challenges of balancing model virtues that *represent* and *reduce* the complexity of the target systems. In this context, standardization of models to improve the reproducibility of results in the laboratory can be counterproductive if the aim is to represent the complexity and variation encountered in the clinic. Practices of animal modeling thus raise fundamental questions about what constitutes good evidence in science and medicine.

Zooming in on specific uses of animals as means for improving human health also exposes important questions about how we relate – physiologically and emotionally – to other species (Sharp 2019; Kiani et al. 2022). The physiological and behavioral similarities between humans and non-human animals simultaneously facilitate translational inferences and produce ethical conflicts. In this sense, epistemic questions about model validity are intertwined with ethical considerations on the weighting of animal welfare and human interests (Singer 1975; Regan 1983). Are such considerations inescapable tensions in animal research, or can caring for experimental animals be reconciled with objectivist norms for good science? Does animal experimentation stabilize the distinctiveness of the human or remind us of the relatedness to other animals?

---

[3] I do not have space to discuss the relationship between human and veterinary medicine. But transfer of knowledge and drug development across these contexts exemplify how some animals can benefit from human medicine – and vice versa (Alder and Easton 2005).

This Element suggests that the methodologies employed in human-directed animal modeling can be a prism through which our understanding of the human is refracted, raising fundamental questions about what defines human nature in comparison to non-human species (Efstathiou 2019; Svendsen 2022, see also Ramsey 2013; 2023).

In zooming in on these issues, the future of animal models must also be critically scrutinized. The perceived necessity and adequacy of animal models in biomedical research and medicine are increasingly contested issues. Critics have for decades stressed how differences between species can lead to misleading inferences, especially when animal models are used to predict the efficacy and adverse effects of drugs (LaFollette and Shanks 1993; 1995). The concerns have been growing with recent studies documenting highly varied translational success of animal modeling (Mullard 2016; Striedter 2022; Swaters et al. 2022). As Leenaars et al. (2019) observe, discussions in the scientific field currently revolve around two main perspectives with different implications for the future of animal models: one explaining the translational failures by suboptimal experimental design and calling for improvements in animal research, and another calling for a radical shift to non-animal methods.

Since the Federal Drug and Cosmetics Act of 1938, animal testing has been a requirement for the protocols of drug development to ensure the safety and efficacy of drugs before they can enter first-in-human trials. But we may currently be witnessing significant changes. In September 2021, the European Parliament almost unanimously voted for an action plan to phase out animal experimentation for research and drug testing (Marshall et al. 2022).[4] The same year, the American Congress passed a bill called the FDA Modernization Act 2.0, which was signed by President Biden in December 2022. The Modernization Act 2.0 removes the strict requirement of animal testing and allows drug developers to use alternative nonclinical tests in drug development.[5] Although it is beyond the scope and purpose of this Element to cover the political and public debates on animal research, the intensified focus on reducing animal experimentation calls for a better understanding of how animal models are used in translational research – and what alternatives there may be for replacing or reducing these. My aim is not to defend a specific view on the future of animal models or the philosophical interpretation of animal models in general, but rather to unpack core questions

---

[4] The aim to phase out animal models in biomedical research was already part of the EU Directive 2010/63, stating that "wherever possible, a scientifically satisfactory method or testing strategy not entailing the use of live animals shall be used" (see also Smith et al. 2013 and Section 6). For more information on the recent action plan, see: www.europarl.europa.eu/news/en/press-room/20210910IPR11926/meps-demand-eu-action-plan-to-end-the-use-of-animals-in-research-and-testing.

[5] www.congress.gov/bill/117th-congress/senate-bill/5002, accessed December 20, 2023.

and considerations that I find important for a nuanced debate. I hope that the Element can provide a conceptual framework to articulate the diversity of epistemic and practical functions of translational models, as well as some of the challenges and proposed solutions in translational research. My aim is also point to questions that I find intriguing but that have not yet received much philosophical attention.

The Element is structured as follows. Section 2 provides introductory reflections on how and whether animals can be said to serve as models in translational research, considering also how animals are constructed or engineered for specific translational purposes. Section 3 explores different aspects of the persistent tension between standardization and variation of animal models. This includes an introduction to the important role of standardized model organisms in translational research but also to the philosophically intriguing roles of non-canonical organisms, including so-called "negative models." With this background, Section 4 revisits the virtues of animal models when these act as "patient substitutes" and stand in for human patients in ways that sometimes blur boundaries between animal model and human patient. Section 5 discusses the epistemic roles of animals in biomedical research that may go beyond the traditional focus on representation in philosophical discussions on models. This involves the temporality of model development and the use of animals as diagnostic tools or as material and collaborative resources. Section 6 discusses the future of animal models, including the potentials and challenges of replacing animal models with non-animal methods, such as in vitro models based on human cells. Finally, Section 7 summarizes the key points and ends with concluding reflections on the need for further philosophical work on the topic of animal models of human disease.

2 Animals as Models of Human Disease

The best material model for a cat is another, or preferably the same cat.
- Rosenblueth and Wiener (1945)

Paraphrasing Rosenblueth and Wiener's famous quote, one might say that in translational research "the best material model of a human is another human, or preferably the same human." In both cases, however, one would misunderstand what a model is. In the broadest sense, a model is a simplified representation of a system or phenomenon that is used to understand, predict, or simulate a real-world behavior or relationship. A more detailed or representationally realistic model is not always better. Rosenblueth and Wiener illustrate this point by referencing Jorge Luis Borges' (1954/1972) fictive story on "exactitude in science," where the science of cartography reaches the highest level of perfection and maps become as big and complex as the landscapes they represent. Such maps are useless because their exact accuracy prevents them from performing their epistemic function as a map, that is, as a simpler overview that helps us navigate in complex spaces. Rosenblueth and Wiener's paper is about the role of theoretical models in science. But animal models can similarly "mediate" between our theoretical understandings of disease mechanisms and a real-world target (Morrison and Morgan 1999) by allowing for more practically accessible or ethically permissible experimental interventions on causal mechanisms. How should the role of animal models be understood in comparison to theoretical models? And are researchers confronted with a similar tension between representing and reducing the complexity of the target? Let us take a closer look at the characteristics of animal models in translational research.

2.1 Modeling Human Disease by Intervening on Animals

The comparison between theoretical models and animal models can be misleading in the sense that we may overlook what makes experimenting on animals special. Levy and Currie (2015) argue that model organisms are not (theoretical) models because they are "samples from, or specimens of, a wider class" (p. 328). Inference from model organisms, they argue, are not made merely through artificially constructed and abstract analogies between model and target. Rather, model organisms are special in providing circumstantial or *phylogenetic* evidence, as members of the same phylogenetic class under investigation (see also Love 2007; Steel 2008; Weber 2005). From this perspective, learning about human diseases by intervening on animals is grounded in the evolutionary conservation of phenotypic traits based on homologous genes and "elementary building blocks" that are universally shared among many organisms (Changeux 2006). Inferences are justified not through idealized approximations but through insights into basic causal features that many organisms have in common. For example, many mechanisms regulating embryonic development appear to be evolutionarily conserved across many species, thus justifying why the neural circuits of an invertebrate such as *Caenorhabditis elegans* can serve as a simple model for neurological disorders in humans (Schaffner 2001). According to Weber (2001; 2005), inferences from such reduced models are justifiable, because biological mechanisms are *hierarchically structured* such that lower-level mechanisms are typically similar across species, even if higher-level capacities differ. From this perspective, extrapolation from interventions on lower-level mechanisms in a different species can be justified if relevant difference-makers can be documented in both contexts.

Undoubtedly, phylogenetic relatedness is important for understanding how interventions on animals can be informative for medicine. Nevertheless, one should be careful not to commit what LaFollette and Shanks (1995) call the modeler's *phylogenetic fallacy*, referring to the uncritical assumption that phylogenetic continuity implies underlying causal similarity. LaFollette and Shanks argue that phylogenetic relatedness cannot justify the use of animal models as *causal analog models*, as phylogenetic relatedness does not justify direct causal inferences. In their view, evolutionary conservation of physiological traits can only support the use of animal models as *hypothetical analog models* to suggest possible mechanisms for further investigation. Indeed, evolutionary conservation of many basic mechanisms does not always extend to homologous links between genes and disease mechanisms or drug metabolism, for example, when comparing the evolution of gene networks and molecular mechanisms in humans and mice (Perlman 2016). Moreover, prior knowledge of disease-relevant causal mechanisms is often not available to guide this exploration of lower-level mechanisms. As Baetu (2016) highlights: "in the initial stages of [translational] research, relying on similarities at the level of the causal structures is of little use, since it is precisely these structures that researchers aim to elucidate" (p. 10). This challenge is sometimes called "the extrapolator's circle" (Steel 2008). In preclinical modeling, the epistemic uncertainty of the translational models is often intertwined with ontological uncertainties about what features of the human disease are most relevant to recapitulate in the model (Green et al. 2022).

The most suitable model must be evaluated through iterative steps, involving not only structural and functional similarities of shared phylogenetic factors or molecular mechanisms but also investigations of what Baetu (2016) calls "symptom similarity," understood as phenotypic features linking animal models to translational targets in experimental interventions. Focusing on symptom similarity can also reveal how the best translational model is not always the phylogenetically closest relative. Chimpanzees are the closest living relatives to humans, with an astonishing 99 percent overlap in protein-coding genetic sequences (Suntsova and Buzdin 2020). Yet, despite the high degree of genetic and physiological similarity, AIDS research in the 1980s and 1990s was confronted with the difficult challenge that HIV-infected chimpanzees did not develop the AIDS-related symptoms seen in humans (van Akker et al. 1994).[6]

---

[6] AIDS-like symptoms and increased mortality have later been observed in wild chimpanzees infected with versions of simian immunodeficiency viruses (Keele et al. 2009). While this finding challenges previous conclusions on species-specific immune adaptations, the example still calls for caution concerning cross-species extrapolation, even when the animal is a "close relative." Chimpanzees have been important animal models in vaccine development (e.g., hepatitis), but invasive research on chimpanzees is now largely prohibited due to ethical concerns (Harding 2017).

These challenges, alongside ethical concerns of using chimpanzees for research, have made researchers explore other animal models, including macaque monkeys infected with simian immunodeficiency viruses, cats infected with feline immunodeficiency virus, and rodent models "humanized" through transgenic techniques to resemble human immune responses. The example of AIDS research thus illustrates how several animal models are often needed, each contributing with some pieces of information to a "mosaic description" of disease mechanisms (Baetu 2016; see also Green 2013; Baetu 2014). Both theoretical and animal modeling therefore involves what Rheinberger nicely formulates as the process of "shuttling back and forth between different spaces of representation" (Rheinberger 1997, pp. 108–109).

Another observation that challenges the strong reliance on justification of model choice via phylogeny is that translational models are no longer limited to the organism's evolutionary features but are often genetically modified to minimize disanalogies to human targets (Maugeri and Blasimme 2011). For example, genetically engineered mouse models (GEMMs) are used to study a variety of diseases including Parkinson's and Alzheimer's disease, Down's syndrome, rheumatoid arthritis, obesity, and diabetes, just like genetically modified porcine models are important animal models in organ and tissue transplantation research (Huber and Keuck 2013; Hardesty 2018; Lowe 2022). According to Parkkinen (2017), it is therefore not possible to distinguish the epistemic strategies of animal and theoretical models with reference to the role of phylogeny alone. Yet, he stresses that this does not challenge the basic claim of Levy and Currie (2015) that theoretical models and animal models serve different epistemic purposes. Parkkinen suggests that a distinction should instead be drawn between theoretical models as *inferential aids* and animal models as *surrogate sources of evidence* (Parkkinen 2017). Drawing on Bolker's (2009) notion of surrogate models (discussed further in Section 4), Parkkinen argues that animal models serve as material surrogates for human patients, making the degree of (material) similarity between model and target more pressing in this context. He contends that: "The more similarities between the model and the target one can establish by whatever means, and the more secure one can be that one's results are not distorted by remaining dissimilarities, the better the model first its role as a stand-in for the target" (p. 496). Indeed, animals are used as models in biomedical research because they are considered sufficiently *biologically like* human counterparts to warrant causal inferences (Lewis et al. 2013), and yet sufficiently *morally different* from humans (Svendsen and Koch 2013). But the notion of "similarity" can be defined in different ways, and what constitutes relevant or sufficient biological similarity (and moral worth) depend also on the historical context and the epistemic purpose of specific studies.

The latter point can be illustrated through a scientific discussion in epilepsy research. In a comment on a study of spontaneous seizures in "epileptic rats" (Nissinen and Pitkänen 2007), Mazarati (2007) distinguishes between what he calls the "analogical modeling approach" and the "conceptual modeling approach." Analogical modeling stresses the representational matching of model and target, akin to what Parkkinen (2017) hints at. From this perspective, the best model to study human epilepsy would be a rodent model *of* epilepsy, that is, a rodent that maximally represents the symptoms and symptom development in the human counterpart (e.g., spontaneous seizures). Conceptual modeling, in contrast, emphasizes that models should not merely resemble targets but should provide easier experimental access to causal factors that cannot be studied without distorting and simplifying the phenomenon of interest (e.g., experimentally induced seizures). Ratti (2020) similarly distinguishes between the notions of "models of" and "models for," where the latter denotes how some models are chosen not because of their direct representational or explanatory force, but because of the interventionist strategies they allow for. In the case of epilepsy research, Mazarati (2007) stresses that "a key rationale underlying the conceptual model is to establish logical relationships among variables rather than simply to account for as many variables as possible. Idealization is a key feature of the conceptual model, allowing for simplification of the phenomenon to such an extent that it can be studied effectively" (Mazarati 2007, p. 112). Mazarati thus points to a relationship between model idealization and practical efficiency (or interventional relevance), not unlike what has also been discussed for (some) theoretical models as "minimal models" (Batterman and Rice 2014).

Mazarati views the conceptual approach to models as superior, but there may be benefits to using both types of models and avoiding generalizations about what constitutes a good translational model, at least if the question is addressed in isolation from specific research questions. A focus on the *validity of the inference* from animal models, given specific aims, may be more fruitful than focusing on the model's similarity to the target. It is common in translational research to distinguish between a model's (i) face validity, (ii) construct (or target) validity, and (iii) predictive validity (Denayer et al. 2014; Lemoine 2015; see also Striedter 2022, p. 21). *Face validity* is emphasized in what Mazarati (2007) calls the analogical modeling approach which emphasizes the similarity of phenotypic traits or symptoms in the model and target "on the face of it." *Construct (or target) validity* refers to similarity relations in the underlying causal mechanisms of a disease-relevant process in a model and a target, which can help explain why a disease occurs or a treatment works and possibly give more reliable predictions (Weber 2001; 2005; Maugeri and Blasimme 2011).[7] Finally, *predictive validity* refers to the reliability of the model to predict outcomes relevant to disease prognosis or treatment. Predictive validity needs not rely on strong representational relations, as some animal models can provide reliable predictions on treatment effects or toxic responses, even if their physiological features do not straightforwardly represent the human body (this will be further discussed in Section 5).

While it is possible to analytically distinguish different types of validity of models, it is by no means straightforward to determine which type of validity is sufficient for a specific purpose, or when a specific model is validated. For example, it is often unclear whether construct validity refers to evidence of possible pathological mechanisms, based on similar causal pathways in animal model and human target, or to more conclusive evidence about the disease mechanisms in both organisms. Further, the evidence status of mechanistic knowledge is, in itself, a topic of wider debate within the philosophy of medicine. Some argue that mechanistic evidence is necessary and perhaps even sufficient for inferences about medical interventions, while others favor statistical evidence from population-based studies (reviewed in Stegenga 2022). Thus, discussions about the validity of animal models go far beyond the question of the extent to which animals are similar to humans. The epistemic uncertainty of inferences from animal models is also intertwined with unresolved questions about what – in general – constitutes good evidence in medicine.

A related point is that for each of the types of validity outlined (face validity, construct validity, and predictive validity), there is an orthogonal dimension of the model's *scope validity*, referring to the scope of the intended targets.[8] While standardized model organisms are intentionally designed to have a broad rep-resentational scope (Ankeny and Leonelli 2020), proponents of so-called *precision medicine* call for preclinical models at the opposite spectrum to better capture the biological variation between patients. In the extreme case, such models may have a scope validity that goes towards one specific patient, for example, when patient-derived xenograft (PDX) models are developed using tumor cells from an individual patient (Green et al. 2021). This topic will be further discussed in Section 4.2.

Generally, the weight given to the specific model features is dependent on the purpose for which an animal model is used. For example, representational

---

[7] As a reviewer helpfully pointed out, the concept of "construct validity" is borrowed from psychology and has a longer history in discussions about what is measured in psychological texts (e.g., Cronbach and Meehl 1955).

[8] I borrow this concept from Lara Keuck, who has used the term "scope validity" in oral presenta-tions to highlight shifting standards in model virtues and evidence in precision medicine.

similarity and face validity can be important for a causal analysis of the natural development of disease symptoms but are sometimes de-emphasized in cases where animals are used primarily as predictive tools for diagnostic purposes or for prediction of treatment effect (Germain 2014; see also Section 5). The aim of this Element is therefore not to define what – in general – constitutes a good translational model. Rather, I hope to introduce a conceptual framework for what animal models do in the pursuit of knowledge on human health. The following section elaborates further on the dimensions of model choice in translational research.

2.2 Dimensions of Model Choice

What constitutes a good translational model is not only a complex epistemic question but also one that involves considerations of practical and ethical issues (Lewis et al. 2013). This is illustrated in a list of criteria for organism choice (Table 1), developed by Dietrich et al. (2020) based on a review of reasons given for organism choice in published scientific literature. I cannot here explain all

Table 1 Different criteria for organism choice stressed in the scientific literature. Adapted from Dietrich et al. (2020).

Cluster	Criterion
Access	(1) Ease of supply
	(2) Phenomenal access
	(3) Ethical considerations
	(4) Standardization
Tractability	(5) Viability and durability
	(6) Responsiveness
	(7) Availability of methods and techniques
	(8) Researcher risks
Resourcing	(9) Previous use
	(10) Epistemic resources
	(11) Training requirements
	(12) Informational resources
Economies	(13) Institutional support
	(14) Financial considerations
	(15) Community support
	(16) Affective and cultural attributes
Promise	(17) Commercial and other applications
	(18) Comparative potential
	(19) Translational potential
	(20) Novelty

criteria in detail, but I have included the table to illustrate the diversity of criteria for organism choice as well as how model criteria can trade off against each other. For example, the translational potential (criteria 19) is high for non-human primates in studies of neurogenerative disorders due to the genetic, physiological, and cognitive similarities with humans. But their use is constrained by other criteria under the clusters called "access" (ease of supply, ethical considerations, and standardization of animal models) and "economies" (financial considerations and affective and cultural attributes). Depending on the weighting of different criteria, rodent models may make up more suitable translational models in neuroscience, although they also have obvious limitations (see Section 2.4 for further discussion). Researchers must therefore often balance considerations of model virtues according to multiple criteria, which can be synergistically or antagonistically related.

Another important point is that many features of organism choice summarized in Table 1 are not simply inherent to animals as "samples of nature" with pre-given epistemic features, such as genetic or physiological similarity to human conditions. Model virtues are also *constructed* through specific historical, social, and technological contexts. As Ankeny stresses, a model system is not just the organism itself, but also the techniques, experimental methodologies, and the research communities surrounding specific animal models (2007, p. 47). The cluster called "resourcing" above is crucial for understanding why some organisms become more widely used than others, as animal experimentation build on previous use of specific models, including institutional efforts to develop specific models via strain collections, databases, and practical expertise (Ankeny and Leonelli 2011; 2020). Organism choice thus also hinges on available laboratory resources, such as specialized manuals and molecular toolkits allowing researchers to selectively breed, house, and experiment on animals, and informational resources such as data infrastructures, where researchers can share data on specific organisms and human conditions of interest. For example, the prominence of the use of zebrafish as translational models is closely tied to institutionalized efforts to map zebrafish orthologs of human genes, for example, through the Zebrafish Information Network (ZFIN) and the HomoloGene database.[9]

Economic and cultural factors are also important for understanding how specific organisms become prominent as translational models or model organisms (criteria 13–16). In situating the historical development of the mouse as a translational model within a broader framework of model organisms, Rader (2004) argues that the mouse models "are the result, rather than

---

[9] See https://zfin.org/ and www.ncbi.nlm.nih.gov/gene/.

the cause, of consensus among early twentieth-century experimental biologists" (p. 15). The title of Rader's book, *Making Mice*, nicely illustrates how the historical development of *Mus musculus* as a translational model requires attention to historically contingent factors associated with the development of laboratory techniques in specific settings and the negotiation of *culturally ingrained* relations between animals and humans. Rader documents how the cultural attitude to mice and rats as pests made it easier for scientists to manage ethical concerns and achieve public support, compared to research on cats and dogs.[10]

Standardization (criteria 4 in Table 1) is key to the process of preclinical model development (Hardesty 2018; Ankeny and Leonelli 2020). Rader shows how the promotion and uptake of the so-called JAX® mice (produced by The Jackson Laboratory, Maine, USA) for medical research in the period from 1900 to 1955 was as dependent on standardization practices of breeding and domestication. The widespread use of the JAX® mice was conditioned on the experimental ability to control genetic variables and reach "genetic purity" of the mouse model. These features were considered central for turning biomedical medicine into a harder science, capable of replicating and reproducing experimental results across different laboratory settings. Rader also highlights how institutional and economic factors influenced the intertwinement of standardization and commercialization of JAX® mice, which were promoted as "biological reagents for diverse lines of medical research" (Rader 2004, p. 7). Inbred mice strains allowed for controlled experiments on transplanted and induced tumors in mice, greatly impacting what was possible in cancer research. Meanwhile, biomedical needs and institutional funding opportunities also framed the development of specific models, which later led to the development of transgenic mouse models that would allow for the manipulation and analysis of specific genes.

A key lesson from the history and philosophy of science is thus that animals are not born as biological models for human disease. Rather, specific animals are chosen partly because of natural attributes and partly because contextual factors allow them to be constructed as human-directed models. Improving the translational potential of models often requires that researchers work actively to minimize disanalogies, for example, when mouse or pig models are "humanized" through gene or stem cell technologies to be compatible with the human immune system (Davies 2010; Lowe 2022). We, therefore, turn next to practices of engineering animal models.

---

[10] Similarly, the extensive use of pigs in public health has been associated with the cultural status of pigs as domesticated animals for consumption in Western countries (Dam and Svendsen 2018; Svendsen 2022).

2.3 Engineering Animal Models

As previously highlighted, model organisms are not merely samples of nature with inherent translational potentials or limitations. Via selective breeding and gene technologies, scientists can actively modify and minimize disanalogies between animal models and human target, making animal models more standardized than wild types and more "like humans." Through such practices, boundaries between humans and animals, and between the natural and artificial, are not only explored but also modified (Sharp 2019). The "engineering epistemology" (Maugeri and Blasimme 2011) in translational research is well illustrated by the existence of different types of mouse models ranging from transgenic disease models, immunocompromised xenograft models with transplanted human tissue, and recent attempts to develop chimeras that not only tolerate but also support a human-like immune system. Each of these models will be briefly discussed.

The development of transgenic models highlights the importance of a model's tractability and responsiveness to genetic manipulation as key factors for organism choice. Experimental interventions on the simple genome of fruit flies, *Drosophila melanogaster*, have historically paved the way for understanding and intervening on many different animals (Kohler 1994; Waters 2008). What Marcel Weber (2005) calls the "molecularization of fruit flies" includes gene knockout strategies and recombinant DNA technology that were later explored in animals with more complex genomes to identify relationships of homolog gene sequences and disease-relevant phenotypes in human and non-human organisms. Challenges for genetic manipulability are similarly important factors for why some models have historically become widespread while others are used less often. Chickens, *Gallus domesticus*, have historically been important animal models in cancer research, for example, in comparative studies of in vitro cultures and in vivo experiments on chick embryos revealing the capacity of living organisms to normalize pathogenic cell phenotypes (Dolberg and Bissell 1984; Stoker et al. 1990). Chickens remain important experimental models in some areas of cancer research, developmental biology, virology, immunology, and epigenetics (Bahr 2008; Beacon and Davie 2021). However, the complexity of chicken genetics has often made biomedical researchers in oncology and human toxicology turn to alternative organisms that are easier to manipulate, such as zebrafish and mice (Ankeny and Leonelli 2020, p. 47). Similarly, the frog *Xenopus tropicalis* has largely replaced *Xenopus laevis* in studies of human genetics and malformations during development, because it has a shorter generation time, lays a larger number of eggs, and has a simpler diploid genome that is easier to manipulate (Grainger 2012; Blum and Ott 2019).

Experimental induction of mutations in mice has been an important strategy in oncology research since the 1980s, where genes identified to be associated with human cancers could make the mouse model more prone to human-like cancers, such as breast cancer (Stewart et al. 1984). For example, many human tumors display mutations in the tumor suppressor gene, p53, and knocking out this gene in mice has provided important information on the various roles of this gene in a cell cycle regulation. The first patented GEMM was the so-called "oncomouse," developed and commercialized in 1988 by researchers at Harvard (Hanahan et al. 2007). Cancer-promoting oncogenes were implanted in mouse embryos of a selectively bred and highly standardized mouse strain via a virus vector, resulting in standardized mouse models with inheritable predispositions for developing tumors that mimic the genetic lesions of human patients. The oncomouse allowed for studying the role of specific hereditary genetic factors in cancer development while keeping environmental factors controlled. But this model system also revealed that multiple interacting genetic factors are involved in tumor development, as even inbred oncomice display variation in the time of cancer development. Parallel to mouse models forming spontaneous tumors, other mouse models were therefore developed to enable control also of the *expressed* disease for testing of treatments. This translational purpose could be supported through allograft models, that is, mice with transplanted tumor tissue from spontaneous tumors developed in other mice.[11]

Later, the translational distance between humans and mice was further reduced through the development of hybrid models. *Hybrid mouse models* can be developed by transplantation of human tumor tissue or injection of human cancer cultures into immunocompromised mice, either under the skin to study solid tumors or in veins to study metastatic tumor growth. Hybrid models are often referred to as xenograft models and can be developed from standardized cancer cell lines or from tumor cells from specific patients (Denayer et al. 2014). The latter are called PDX models and have been highlighted as key tools for precision medicine to recapitulate the variation in the tumor types of specific patients (see Section 4.2). New developments in genome editing, such as CRISPR-mediated genome editing, present further options for actively creating analogies and minimizing disanalogies between animal models and human targets (Russell et al. 2017). As Maugeri and Blasimme (2011) argue, although genome editing is conditioned on and constrained by phylogenetic homologies, the "naturalized epistemology" of the homology view is insufficient to capture the role of engineered translational models. This calls for further philosophical

---

[11] To minimize immune rejection, transplantation of tumors can also be done between mice of the same strain (commonly called isograft models).

reflections on what constitutes boundaries between specifies and the extent to which these are modifiable.

In the exploration of human–animal boundaries, the immune system presents an interesting frontier that separates different species or even individuals (Davies 2012). Yet, even this boundary is plastic, as researchers are attempting to construct a human-like immune system in rodents and pigs to allow for more adequate studies of autoimmune diseases, HIV, cancer immune therapies, and xenotransplantation (Kalscheuer et al. 2012; De La Rochere et al. 2018; Lowe 2022). But despite progress in constructing human-like immune cells via stem cell transplantation and reprogramming of adult stem cells, developing mice with human-like immune systems remains a difficult task. Among the challenges are low engraftment rates of hematopoietic stem cells in mice and difficulties maintaining the human immune cells in the adaptive immune system of the murine model over time. Moreover, it is not straightforward to experimentally distinguish between what is a human-like immune response and an animal-like allogenic (rejection) response (Davies 2012; Allen et al. 2019; Green et al. 2021). The view that animal models are *engineered* does, therefore, not imply that the translational distance between animal model and human target is fully bridged. Moreover, as discussed in the next section, the process of translation is often not a straightforward process to make models resemble fixed targets.

2.4 Extrapolation, Transposition, and Epistemic Scaffolding

The term "extrapolation" is widely used to describe the process of using data obtained in controlled animal studies as evidence in human biomedical contexts (e.g., Burian 1993; Schaffner 1986; 2001; Steel 2008; Piotrowska 2013; Baetu 2016). But even scholars using the term have stressed that the term is potentially misleading. Extrapolation is a term borrowed from mathematics, where functions fitted from observed data are extended to situations outside the scope of observation, for example, through a projection of current tendencies onto the future. But as Weber (2001) contends, "extrapolation" misleadingly indicates that the strength of translational inferences is not open to further empirical investigation. The mathematical language of "extrapolation" or "inference" may therefore be inadequate for capturing the complex inferential connections established between animal models and human targets in translational research. For example, Ankeny (2001) describes the role of model organisms in genomics as a form of "case-based reasoning" involving multidirectional feedback loops between different model systems, which can involve coordinated research on different species. Given this complexity, scholars using the term "extrapolation" often explicate that inferences involve multiple iterative loops between model and target (Panksepp 1998; Changeux 2006; Baetu 2016). Yet, others suggest that a different or additional conceptual framework is needed.

Friese and Clarke (2012) use the term *transposition* to stress how animal models create dynamic and iterative connections between different things. In their view, transposition better covers the social processes of "moving knowledge, techniques, and bodies to different places and contexts" (Friese and Clarke 2012, p. 45). Transposition does not collapse differences between bodies or species, but it can destabilize and transform the relations between these. Friese and Clarke illustrate this through the need for "simplification work" (Star 1983) in the history of reproductive science to de-emphasize species differences between non-human primates and humans. They for instance describe how alignment of data on the menstrual cycle in humans and non-human primates required omitting data from primates during months where the cycle was season dependent. Friese and Clarke also emphasize how transposition from studies on rhesus monkeys in the 1920s required infrastructural work on the clinical side. In this case, a parallel study collecting data from vaginal smears and women's self-reporting on menses were required to draw "human bodies into the scientific enterprise by association" (Friese and Clarke 2012, p. 38). The framework offered by Friese and Clarke thus emphasizes the need for infrastructural work on both the preclinical and clinical side to allow for selective comparisons and transpositions.

Further building on the notion of transposition, Lowe (2022) similarly stresses the *mediating iterativity* of translational animal research. In the historical development of translational pig models for diabetes research, techniques and knowledge were transposed not only from animal research to human medicine but also in the opposite direction. For example, the application of human genomics techniques to research on pigs revealed an unknown mutation in a gene called RN, informally known as the "acid-meat" gene because it is linked to excess glycogen in the muscles (and a low pH). Subsequent identification of the corresponding mutation in humans led to new insights into the genetic background for non-insulin diabetes. Rather than depicting the human genome as a predetermined and fixed reference point for translational research via the pig genome, Lowe argues that transposition required "continual testing and refinement of the models of correspondences between the genomes of the two species" (Lowe 2022, p. 66). He also emphasizes that the very criteria of homology were co-constructed in this process, which involves collaborations between the pre-existing communities of pig and human geneticists (see also García-Sancho and Lowe 2023). The intertwined history of human and pig genomics thus also illustrates the importance of (non-translational) animal research for biomedical science.

Another important conceptual reframing of the role of animals in biomedical research is provided by Nelson's analysis of animal experimentation in the field of animal behavior genetics (2013; 2018). Nelson argues that the notions of "extrapolation" and "translation" leave the interactions between the model and the modeled as a blind spot and give the impression that the aim of animal models is to account for the full complexity of the human condition. Yet, as she points out, scientists are painstakingly aware of the difficulties of studying complex phenomena such as human anxiety, depression, or memory in rodent models. A further problem with "extrapolation," according to Nelson, is that it presupposes that the modeled target stays stable and certain during the modeling process. This is often not the case when dealing with complex diseases, such as psychiatric disorders. Drawing on ethnographic fieldwork, Nelson studies how disagreements in the clinical profession about the evidence status of behavioral tests using mice are entangled with uncertainty and disagreement about how human anxiety should be defined or "measured." To better capture the complexity of the dynamics of inference between animal model and target system, she suggests the notion of "epistemic scaffolding."

"Epistemic scaffolding" is intended to capture how supporting structures for evidence relations between animal models and human targets can be built up but also weakened or broken down as research progresses. The strength of evidence relations can be adjusted to "different heights," depending on the perceived strength of the model system. This is illustrated in Figure 1, using the relationship between human anxiety and the "elevated plus maze" test on rodents as an example. The elevated plus maze consists of an elevated plane with four arms. Two arms have enclosed walls and the other two lead into open spaces. The maze presents the mice with a conflict situation between their opposing instincts to explore novel environments and avoid open spaces to reduce exposure to predators. The maze was proposed in the 1980s to model human anxiety disorders by considering disordered behavior and reluctance to explore "open arms" as a proxy for human anxiety. It was found that drugs known to decrease human anxiety can increase the time mice spend on the "open arms" of the maze, thus making the maze a possible testbed for anxiolytic drug development. Yet, the broken lines on the figure indicate the instability of these relations, as the behavior cannot easily be related to human anxiety. Specifically, it is debated whether the maze test can be used to distinguish between normal and pathological avoidance behaviors. Nelson analyzes how discussions of these issues among neuroscientists often lead to reconfiguration of parts of the epistemic scaffold. Rather than abandoning the animal model test system entirely, they signal the instability by avoiding direct

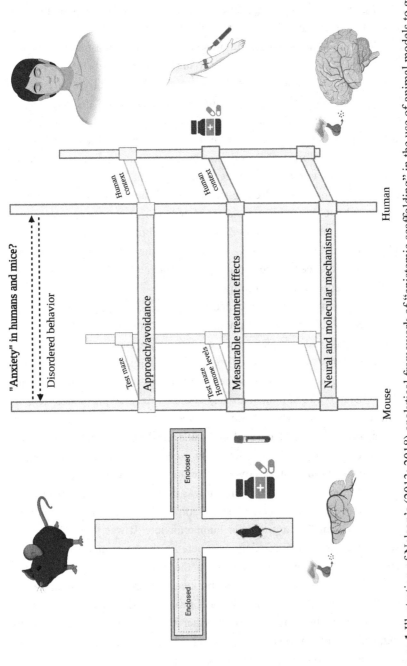

Figure 1 Illustration of Nelson's (2013; 2018) analytical framework of "epistemic scaffolding" in the use of animal models to gain information about treatments against human anxiety. The figure was created by the author with BioRender.com.

comparisons between mental states in humans and animals, for example, by using the more cautious language of "anxiety-like behavior" in the context of mice.

A common strategy to manage this epistemic uncertainty is to focus on simpler behavioral symptoms and their underlying biology. Evidence relations are established not only by advancing and combining models to achieve symptom similarity in model and target but also by methodologically *reconfiguring the target* (human disorders). This is for instance done through decomposition of the complex phenomenon into smaller or simpler units of analysis. Weber (2001) similarly highlights that what is often framed as an "extrapolation question" is strongly intertwined with the issue of reductionism in the sense that "the possibility of generalizing from a simple system to a more complex one depends on the extent to which the behavior of complex systems can be explained by the properties of their parts" (p. 236). For Weber, the stability of inferences thus rests on the possibility of reducing or decomposing human conditions into conserved molecular mechanisms that can be studied in animal models. Nelson (2018) elaborates further on this through attention to how neuroscientists sometimes use the notion of *endophenotype models*. These models capture only selected elements of a disorder or phenomenon of interest through more narrowly defined quantifiable measures, for example, a pathway, symptom, or treatment effect first identified in humans (see also Kendler and Neale 2010). The instability of the top of the epistemic scaffold in Figure 1 does therefore not shake the foundation of model use.

Drawing on cases in translational psychiatry, Lemoine (2015) similarly argues that what is "lost in translation" is not primarily the similarity of the rodent model and the target, but the indeterminacies of the target condition in humans. Because mental disorders are "fuzzy targets" to begin with, scientists resort to piecemeal theorizing about lower-level mechanisms and a *treatment-driven* approach via endophenotype models. If this underlying "scaffold" is sufficiently strong, the utility of animal experimentation does not hinge directly on whether the mouse experiences anxiety or depression in a "human sense." Rather, it depends on whether the endophenotypic behavior in the animal model accurately predicts anxiolytic effects in humans. In other words, construct validity and predictive validity can sometimes be established, even if many aspects of the model lack face validity. Lemoine illustrates this with the example of the so-called Tail Suspension Test for a drug's effect on depression. Obviously, testing whether laboratory mice stop moving when their tail is suspended has limited "face validity" as a representation of human depression. But what matters is the predictive power and reliability of the test result. The predictive power will, however, hinge on regularities between shared molecular mechanisms and functional phenotypic traits. Thus, questions about the validity of specific animal models and animal experiments are often intertwined with questions about the possibility and limitations of reductive mechanistic explanations (Weber 2001; 2005). Animal modeling in the context of mental disorders is particularly difficult, not only because we lack insights to "what it is like to be a rodent" in a behavioral test (Genzel 2021), but also because the diagnostic criteria for the human conditions are complex and ill-defined.

To sum up, inferences in human-directed modeling often go in multiple directions, and not only from an animal model to a fixed human target. Treatment effects or possible mechanisms are sometimes identified first in humans and subsequently explored through interventions in rodent models, where genes can be knocked out to study effects on altered hormonal pathways and neurological mechanisms. Such results can sometimes be successfully linked to human test results. But when challenges occur, epistemic scaffolds may be broken down or reconstructed via refinement of the animal model or testing procedures, a process sometimes referred to as "back translation" (e.g., Denayer et al. 2014). In some cases, instability of the scaffold is based on or lead to uncertainties about the defining features of human conditions. We explore this topic further in the following section.

2.5 Reverse Translation and Target Instability

The previous section highlighted the iterative and dynamic relationships between animals and humans in biomedical research, allowing for inferences to go in multiple directions. This reciprocity of knowledge transfer between animal model and human target is sometimes referred to as "forward" and "reverse translation" by practicing scientists. While forward translation refers to inferences from animal model to human target, reverse translation goes in the opposite direction. More specifically, reverse translation refers to the strategy of starting with knowledge from human trials and developing animal models that mimic these conditions to explore underlying mechanisms. The importance of reverse translation has been stressed in stroke research, where human data from hematoma samples have been used to identify subpopulations based on the characteristics of white blood cells, and subsequent work in mouse models was used to identify molecular pathways that were later verified in human patients (Bix et al. 2018). Reverse translation has also been proposed to improve addiction research, where scientists have called for different animal models to account for differences in treatment needs. Because some patients with addiction problems may respond better to specific forms of treatment (e.g., opioid maintenance treatment, psychotherapeutic treatment, or a community-reinforcement approach), some suggest that rodent models should be developed to mimic responsiveness to specific treatment types (Venniro et al. 2020). This form of reverse translation hinges on the hope that different animal models of successful treatments can help identify underlying mechanisms of action, which can then be "forward" translated to refine and further develop treatments.

Animal modeling in addiction research is particularly intriguing from a philosophical perspective, because the very ability to model the complexity of addiction problems in non-human animals is contested. It is generally accepted that the physiological *effects* of substance dependence can be modeled in animals, for example, through experimental injection of drugs or alcohol and subsequent observation of metabolic readouts, organ function, and behavioral capacities in comparison to a control group. But it is more controversial whether the physiological and psychological *causes* of human addiction problems and behaviors can be accounted for in animal models. For instance, the aim of making animals "alcoholic" is confronted with the challenge that animals do not easily become "addicted" via voluntary oral intake of drugs or alcohol. Most animals (including monkeys, cats, dogs, and rodents) simply refuse to drink alcohol if it is not experimentally induced. Ankeny et al. (2014) and Ramsden (2015) provide fascinating historical analyses of how the "determined sobriety" among rodents has forced researchers to develop different *environmentally situated* models of alcohol addiction. Also in this context, discussions about the evidence status of the animal models are intertwined with competing perspectives on the human condition (alcoholism).

Experimental strategies to make rodents drink alcohol include offering alcohol while depriving them of food and/or water, adding a sucrose solution to ethanol to modify the taste, as well as a strategy called "schedule-induced polydipsia." The latter draws on operant conditioning, that is, a strategy to modify animal behavior through learned expectations of rewards. Intermittent feeding of small food pellets to rats at short intervals has been found to increase their intake of water. Operant conditioning can similarly make rats drink large amounts of alcohol resembling "binge drinking" in humans. Yet, it has been questioned whether the experimentally induced behavior corresponds to human intoxication and craving for alcohol. The concern is that what is modeled in rodents is a behavior associated with the animal's craving for a food reward. The rats may drink alcohol simply because the expected reward and preferred behavior (eating) is not available to them. Similarly, making rats drink alcohol by adding sweeteners to alcohol makes it difficult to distinguish the rodents' motivation for drinking and for caloric intake.

Interestingly, however, what some see as confounding factors are by others interpreted as conditions akin to how humans start drinking alcohol. Humans are typically not first exposed to hard liquor but instead to mixed drinks, and environmental stress and operant conditioning in animals may also bear resemblance to relevant mechanisms in human alcoholism (Ankeny et al. 2014). Ramsden (2015) discusses how controversies around the translational potential of rat models developed via operant conditioning sparked renewed interest in and debate about the *environmental causes* of human alcoholism. From one perspective in this debate, animals could only be relevant translational models for human alcoholism if they drink ethanol solutions excessively, chronically, and consistently *independently* of environmental variations. But from competing perspectives highlighting environmental causes of alcoholism, behavioral changes in drinking patterns according to environmental triggers better corresponds to how alcoholism is a human response to environmental conditions (socioeconomic causes, traumas, pain, etc.) and the absence of behavioral alternatives (Ramsden 2014, p. 186). Rather than viewing alcoholism primarily as a physical or psychological disease at the individual level, the environmentally situated model was instructive for reconceptualizing alcoholism as a symptom or result of *harmful environments*. This reconceptualization also had important implications for possible interventions to prevent or counteract the chronicity of human addiction problems. The example thus nicely illustrates how diverging laboratory approaches to animal models can reflect and impact shifting historical perspectives on human diseases.

The intertwinement of model uncertainty and target instability may be particularly apparent in animal research on mental disorders and addition, but the relevance of this point is broader. Debates in cancer research on the epistemic features of preclinical models are intertwined with ontological uncertainty about how – and at what organizational level – cancer should be defined. Researchers for instance debate the extent to which cancer can be recapitulated in *in vitro* organoids or require the physiological complexity of whole-organism in vivo systems (see Section 6). Similarly, debates about the benefits and challenges of standardized animal models and cancer cell lines reflect uncertainties about the level of variation in the classification of cancer types and subtypes (Green et al. 2021; 2022). In the following, we explore further how animal-based translational research is confronted with persistent tensions between standardization and variation.

3 Balancing Standardization and Variation

3.1 Model Organisms in Translational Research

Most translational research and drug testing is, as mentioned, conducted on a small set of standardized model organisms. The leading model organisms in biomedical research are rodents, especially *M. musculus* and *Rattus norvegicus.* The prevalence of each of these models in recent decades have been highly associated with the development of genome-editing tools, first for mice and later for rats (Ellenbroek and Yuon 2016). While the mammalian model of choice for many diseases is still the mouse model, rats are commonly used for pharmaceutical and toxicological testing, as well as for studies of complex traits such as cardiovascular and diabetes research, arthritis, and neuroscience experiments requiring an animal with highly goal-oriented behavior and capacity of rule learning (Szpirer 2020; Genzel 2021).[12] Other important model organisms in translational research include non-mammalian vertebrates, such as zebrafish and frogs, and invertebrate models such as nematodes and fruit flies. While these models are physiologically and phylogenetically more distant from humans, these models have practical advantages, such as easier experimental manipulability, lower costs, and shorter generation times.

What constitutes a model organism is not just the inherent biological features or the number of specimens used, but also the institutional structures of repositories focusing on specific model systems (Ankeny and Leonelli 2011; 2020). Important resources include gene ontology databases, "mutant libraries," and stock collections. Gene ontologies contain structured and standardized data, which can be used to identify homologue (disease-relevant) genes in humans and animal models (Leonelli and Ankeny 2012). The databases are often hierarchically linked in the sense that more specialized databases contribute to broader gene ontologies, with the GO Consortium as the largest one.[13] Many databases integrate information on specific model organisms. For example, the Mouse Genome Informatics (MGI)[14] database, hosted by The Jackson Laboratory, integrates data from more specialized databases developed by the same institution and partners working on mouse models. The MGI is an important resource for ontology in particular,[15] but this database also contains a "Disease Ontology Browser," where data on a range of different diseases studied in mice and humans are integrated via "gene-to-disease" mappings.[16] Similarly, the Rat Genome Database (RGD) is a repository for structured research data on rats, which can be accessed via searches on specific genes or via "Disease Portals"

---

[12] Rats are often favored over mice in cardiovascular research, because the larger body size makes it possible to conduct additional types of tests and serial blood draws (Szpirer 2020).

[13] http://geneontology.org/, accessed December 30, 2023.

[14] www.informatics.jax.org/, accessed December 30, 2023.

[15] The Jackson Laboratory hosts the Mouse Models of Human Cancer database (MMHCdb), containing curated resources of data from various mouse models of human cancers, as well as repositories of inbred and genetically engineered mouse strains.

[16] This initiative is called the Human-Mouse: Disease Connection (HMDC), www.informatics.jax .org/disease.

providing genetic and phenotypic information on many different diseases.[17] Other important databases for translational research include the ZFIN database (The Zebrafish Information Network), the WormBase (containing annotated genomes and neural networks representations of *C. elegans* and other nematodes), and FlyBase (the primary repository for data on *D. melanogaster*). Some databases are also disease-specific and integrate data from several organisms. An example is FaceBase,[18] an NIH-supported initiative to integrate data from omics analyses and morphometric studies of dental, oral, and craniofacial research on humans, mice, and zebrafish. In addition to gene ontologies, mutant libraries and stock collections are important resources for translational model development, containing manuals and techniques for genome editing as well as standardized strains representing specific diseases can be ordered and shipped to different laboratories (Striedter 2022).

Since another Cambridge Element discusses what is special about model organisms (Ankeny and Leonelli 2020), I focus on considerations about the translational benefits and drawbacks of the intensified focus on a small subset of standardized animal models that are selectively bred. Model organisms are well suited for concerted efforts to understand the basic biology of a variety of diseases and provide standardized and controlled materials for experimental studies where reproducibility is important. As Ankeny and Leonelli (2020) put it, model organisms are "transformed into models within highly standardized, uniform, and simplified environments, which because of their 'placelessness' can function as anchors for a broad and ever-evolving modelling ecosystem" (p. 19). But the focus on uniform animal models has also raised concerns about their translational potential and missed opportunities for translational research.

Würbel (2002) uses the notion of the "standardization fallacy" to denote the failure to acknowledge how strategies to optimize the *internal validity* of translational animal experiments (e.g., reproducibility within the laboratory) come at the expense of *external validity* (e.g., reproducibility of results in clinical settings with heterogenous populations or environments). While standardization increases the comparability, replicability, and reproducibility of experiments on preclinical animal models, these practices may come at the expense of leaving the impact of biological and environmental variation unexplored. As Logan (2002) highlights, selective breeding of model organisms promoted the belief that many species were fundamentally similar, and "scientific generality became an a priori assumption rather than an empirical conclusion" (p. 329). This challenges of standardization will be further unpacked through examples.

---

[17] https://rgd.mcw.edu/rgdweb/portal/index.jsp, accessed December 30, 2023.
[18] www.facebase.org/, accessed December 30, 2023.

One potential blind spot resulting from the standardization fallacy is the understudied (and thus largely unknown) impact of intra-species variation on the translational success of a tested drug. Variation among the specimens in a panel of animal models is typically avoided through selective breeding and genetic engineering to control for confounding factors and improve reproducibility in the lab. But the reliance on inbred strains come with the risk that the inferences drawn are highly model-specific, thus compromising the external validity of animal models. This concern is illustrated in a study on mouse models for Ebola research, published in *Science* (Rasmussen 2014). The paper outlines how the preferred translational model, *M. musculus*, has traditionally been considered limited for Ebola research, because of the lack of relevant symptoms (hemorrhagic fever) in standard laboratory mice.[19] This feature may, however, be a characteristic of specific laboratory mice strains rather than mice in general. To explore the impact of host genetic variation on virus response, the authors developed a spectrum of genetically different mouse models via crossbreeding. In the expanded mouse model panel, Ebola-infection led to a striking variation in the pathogenic phenotypes, ranging from complete resistance to infection to lethal infection with and without symptoms. These results were good news for the potential of comparative studies of different strains of mouse models in Ebola research (for a historical review and recent updates, see Bradfute 2023). However, the result also underscores the risk that many results in translational research could be contingent on the genetic background of specific model strains, which do not resemble the genetic variation among target patients. Similar worries are seen in cancer research, and some scholars have called for more systematic repetition of experimental findings in different types of mouse models (Denayer et al. 2014, p. 6).

Another concern is that the widespread use of a few selected model organisms limits the possibilities for knowledge generation. While results of standardized model organisms are easier to compare and reproduce across laboratories, they may also leave many possibilities unexplored. Burian (1993) frames the concern as an innate bias reflected in an "unwillingness to consider the entire biologic kingdom as a source of possible models" (p. 351). Beery and Kaufer (2015) similarly argue that biomedical research on neurobiology is "biased towards rats and mice" (p. 117), which constitute about 90 percent of the mammalian models used. In the context of developmental biology, Bolker and Raff (1997) also stress that the prominence of fruit flies, worms, and mice constrains the type of research

---

[19] Alternative models such as macaque monkeys, guinea pigs, and hamsters do exhibit similar symptoms, but these models come with other challenges, such as ethical concerns and fewer genomic resources to draw on.

that can be conducted (see also Bolker 2012; 2017). Using a broader spectrum of animal models could potentially lead to new insights and more robust inferences.

The designation of 13 specific species as model organisms by the National Institutes of Health (NIH) in 1990 has also caused worries about a negative relationship between focused biomedical funding and diversity of model organisms in research. While it is difficult to isolate the impact of funding and other factors influencing model choice, it is interesting to note that empirical studies do not confirm the concern about declining model diversity (Dietrich et al. 2014; Erick Peirson et al. 2017). Still, it may be true that "studying only a few organisms limits science to the answers that those organisms can provide" (Bolker 2012, p. 31). We therefore next turn to the use of non-canonical animal models.

3.2 Non-canonical Animal Models and Krogh Organisms

The need for non-canonical animal models is in the scientific literature often stressed in relation to the shortcomings of traditional model organisms. For example, aging research often rely on *C. elegans* as a model system, because many genetic modifications associated with aging are evolutionarily conserved and well known, and because their short lifespan of nematodes "speeds up" the experimental process. However, invertebrates generally lack an adaptive immune system, and translational inferences about age-related diseases often require additional experiments on vertebrate models. Yet, studies on standard vertebrate models (such as rodents) are resource-demanding due to their long lifespan. To bridge between the model virtues of existing model organisms, the African turquoise killifish, *Nothobranchius furzeri,* has been proposed as an alternative (Valenzano et al. 2017). The killifish is the shortest-lived vertebrate that still displays relevant aging phenotypes, including age-dependent cancer, within months rather than years. Aging researchers also stress the benefits of mapping differences in homolog genes and age-related diseases across a wide array of species with different lifespans, which is increasingly becoming possible with comparative genomics (Russell et al. 2017). It is also interesting to note that the RGD has recently expanded to become a "multispecies knowledgebase" (Smith et al. 2020), including data on eight additional species, some of which are not typically considered model organisms (e.g., chinchilla, dog, bonobo, 13-lined squirrel, green monkey, and the naked mole rat).[20]

When justifying the choice of a non-standard animal model, scientists often refer to the Krogh principle. This refers to a statement by the Danish physiologist and Nobel laureate August Krogh (1874–1949), who claimed that "[f]or such a large number of problems there will be some animal of choice, or a few such

---

[20] https://rgd.mcw.edu/wg/about-us/, accessed December 20, 2023.

animals, on which it can be most conveniently studied" (Krogh 1929). Krogh suggested that physiological mechanisms were best identified through comparative studies in humans and a range of non-human animals, as illustrated in his own work on respiratory physiology by studying frogs, eels, pigeons, tortoises, and so on (Larsen 2021).[21] Krogh's favorite example of experimental convenience was a specific tortoise, *Testudo graeca*, which he jokingly claimed to be "specially adapted" for experiments on pulmonary function:

> Many years ago when my teacher, Christian Bohr, was interested in the respiratory mechanism of the lung and devised the method of studying the exchange through each lung separately, he found that a certain kind of tortoise possessed a trachea dividing into the main bronchi high up in the neck, and we used to say as a laboratory joke that this animal had been created expressly for the purposes of respiration physiology (Krogh 1929, pp. 202–203).

Krogh stressed that the experimental procedure necessary to measure gas exchange in the two lungs would be "rather difficult to perform on mammals, and may vitiate the results by injuring the animal" (Krogh 1910, p. 202). In contrast, the bronchi in the tortoise could be experimentally accessed along the whole length of its neck, and tubes could be inserted "with the greatest facility, and the animal is practically not injured at all" (see also Wang 2011). Similarly, Krebs (1975) illustrates how this heuristic principle guided the widespread use of the *Loligo* squid in neurobiology, because it has an unusually thick axon that can easily be dissected and studied in isolation. Krebs also highlights how his own work on oxidative metabolism (and his discovery of the citric acid cycle) benefitted from this principle for organism choice, as he chose to experiment on the flight muscle in pigeons which has an unusually high metabolic activity. Other examples of experimental convenience include organisms with transparent eggs or embryos that allow developmental researchers to visually track developmental stages (Burggren 1999; Burggren and Warburton 2007).

The Krogh principle highlights the importance of experimental access to biological mechanisms that are distinctively displayed in specific animal model systems, but "convenience" is a broad term that in the scientific literature is used to highlight rather diverse model virtues (Dietrich et al. 2020). What, then,

---

[21] Krogh is particularly known for his discovery of the capillary regulatory mechanisms of blood perfusion in muscles and organs, as well as experimental documentation of how gas exchange in the lungs occurs through passive diffusion (Schmidt-Nielsen 1995/2019). Krogh also introduced insulin production in Denmark to help patients with type-I diabetes, including his wife and scientific collaborator (Marie Krogh). This laid the foundation for Novo Nordisk to become the world's largest producer of insulin. Interestingly, the use of insulin in treatment was initially developed via extraction of insulin from a dog's pancreas by Canadian researchers. A brief historical overview can be accessed here: www.novonordisk.com/about/insulin-100-years.html, accessed December 20, 2023.

distinguishes a "Krogh organism" from a model organism? According to Love (2010), Krogh organisms differ from model organisms in being selected with a specific problem-focus in mind, rather than aiming for a broad representational scope. When a specific physiological problem is the starting point, organisms with an *unusual* physiology often become more relevant, either because their specific physiological structures is practically convenient for laboratory experiments or because organisms with extreme adaptations most clearly illustrate physiological solutions to environmental challenges. For example, Krogh suggested that the basic mechanisms of kidney function could be best identified through a comparison of kidney morphology and renal function in diverse organisms. Although the kidneys of organisms adapted to, say, a life in a dry dessert do not resemble human kidneys, these organisms are physiologically interesting because the regulatory mechanisms are more distinctively displayed in organisms adapted to an environment with scarce water resources (Green et al. 2018). Comparative physiology thus draws on the productive tension between assumed generality of basic mechanisms and the observed diversity of organisms. Yet, the Krogh principle should be considered only as a heuristic for organism choice (Logan 2002).

Krogh organisms illustrate how some organisms can be chosen because specific traits of interests are different from standard model organisms or even different from humans. An extreme case is when an organism is chosen because of the *absence* of a human physiological problem. Such organisms are often called *negative models*. Although these can be considered as a special category of Krogh organisms (Green et al. 2018), I have chosen to discuss these in a separate section.

3.3 Negative Models of Human Disease

Negative models are in scientific textbooks defined as "species, strains, or breeds in which a certain disease does not develop, e.g., gonococcal infection in rabbits following an experimental treatment that induces the diseases in other animal(s)" (Hau 2008, p. 5). Negative models are animals that do not naturally develop diseases or physiological problems seen in humans or traditional model organisms. Like the example of gonococcal-resistant rabbits, pangolins and bats have been interesting for research on vaccines and treatments against Covid-19, because they are unusually resistant to coronaviruses (Stegman 2021). The main motivation for using such "negative models" in research on infective disease is to explore possible mechanisms of disease resistance that could be utilized in the development of treatments or vaccines. Similarly, to identify preventive and therapeutic strategies for patients with heart failure, preserved ejection fraction, and exercise intolerance, it can be medically relevant to explore what cardiovascular mechanisms allow giraffes to cope with extreme blood pressure changes, when moving their long necks up and down (Horowitz et al. 2020).

The term "negative model" is not uncontroversial. In response to Green et al. (2018), Stegman (2021, p. 14) finds it misleading to construe organisms with pathology-resistant features as "negative models," because the mechanisms of interest – per definition – cannot be generalized or extrapolated to humans. Rather than using the term "model" in this context, Stegman suggests the term "medical toolkit organisms." This term nicely captures the application-oriented interests in specific organisms. Yet, I am not convinced that this terminology is better. First, the concept of a negative model is already used in the scientific literature and usefully highlights how non-canonical models are identified in comparison to animals that *positively* display human-like diseases. Naked mole rats are prime examples of negative models because their physiology at first sight appears physiologically to traditional mouse models, and yet they are long-lived and strikingly resistant to cancer and other age-related diseases. The scientific puzzles posed by "negative models" are thus comparatively defined. Moreover, it is not always possible to reduce the function of negative models to the instrumental role of "medical tools," as also illustrated through the example of the naked mole rat.

Naked mole rats, *Heterocephalus glaber*, display several physiological superpowers and behaviors that are very uncharacteristic of mammals. Naked mole rats were awarded the *Science* price of the "Vertebrate of the Year" in 2013, but they have received scientific attention by taxonomists and zoologists for more than 150 years. The burrowing rodent from eastern Africa were initially studied primarily because their unusual eusocial behaviors resemble the collaborative and hierarchical social structures seen in ant or bee colonies (Buffenstein et al. 2012). Laboratory studies of naked mole rats also made them interesting for physiologists, because they seemingly thrive in harsh and oxygen-deprived underground environments. And despite their wrinkled appearance, naked mole rats have the rodent record in longevity (<35 years), and they are extremely resistant to pain and almost immune to cancer (Gorbunova et al. 2020). Accordingly, naked mole rats are interesting not only from the perspective of comparative physiology but also for translational research on cancer and aging.

One important explanation for the resistance to aging and cancer in naked mole rats, reported in a publication in *Nature* in 2013, is that they have very high-molecular-weight hyaluronan (vHMW-HA) (Tian et al. 2013). Hyaluronan is an important component in the extracellular matrix in most tissues. The polymer length and molecular mass of this glycosaminoglycan influence the biochemical properties of tissues, which impact cell signaling and tumor development (Gorbunova et al. 2020). Insights from genetic studies of naked mole rats have led to suggestions for new cancer therapies targeting an HA-induced receptor, a pathway involving conserved tumor suppressor proteins, and a protein isoform hypothesized to induced cell-cycle arrest (reviewed in Rankin and Frankel 2016). So far, vHMW-HA has only been found to naturally exist in naked mole rats but is used clinically as injections against osteoarthritis, and different forms of hyaluronan are now also found in creams that treat skin burns, inflammation, infections, and wrinkles (Gorbunova et al. 2020). Research on naked mole rats thus illustrates how the absence of a human disease in animals can be useful for treatment development. But insights from naked mole rats do not just have instrumental value. Rather, this research contributes also to basic research in physiology, cancer, and aging. Specifically, research on the role of vHMW-HA has provided insights into the causal role of soft matter tissue properties in cancer development, thus challenging a reductive definition of cancer as a genetic disease defined at the molecular or cellular level (Rankin and Frankel 2016; Green 2021).

Regenerative medicine is another area of research where negative models are very important. The capacities of the human body to recover from serious injuries are very limited, but some animals can regrow entire limbs, whole organs, and even parts of the central nervous system (CNS). For example, it is hoped that research into the mechanisms of CNS regeneration in lampreys and axolotls can help identify new treatment strategies for spinal cord injuries and tissue regeneration (Russell et al. 2017; Maxson Jones and Morgan 2023). Examples from regenerative medicine also illustrate how negative models need not always be exotic or unusual animals. An intriguing example is the use of zebrafish hearts as a negative model for development of gene therapies for heart tissue repair in humans. Human hearts lack stem cells and cannot recover from tissue damage such as cell death following arterial thrombosis. Zebrafish, in contrast, retain the capacity to regenerate heart tissue throughout their whole lifetime (Ellman et al. 2021). A new research project has identified the genetic basis for this capacity in zebrafish hearts, and it is hoped that gene therapies for humans can be developed via modification of the homologue human gene (Bjernemose 2023). If successful, gene therapies are planned to be conducted first in mice (via viral transfer of homologue mouse gene) before similar procedures can be considered in humans. This example also illustrates how experiments on "negative" and "positive" models are often combined to identify possible disease-resistant mechanisms and treatment options.

3.4 Where the Wild Things Are: Reconsidering Laboratory Standards

The previous sections discussed the benefits of using standardized model organisms versus non-canonical models such as Krogh organisms and negative models. Another issue concerns implications of *laboratory standards* for translational research. As Ankeny and Leonelli (2020, p. 24) emphasize, the biggest source of uniformity in model organisms research is due to the standardization of laboratory environments, since variation in temperature, nutrients, lighting, and other factors are limited and highly controlled in model organism research. While laboratory standards are essential to gain experimental control of parameters and enhance comparability and reproducibility of results, the artificial conditions also raise concerns about the translatability of results outside laboratory contexts.

Waters (2008) stresses that discussions about what warrants inferences from the laboratory to other contexts is as important as discussions about inferences across species. Drawing on the historical case of studies of inheritance in fruit flies, he emphasizes that experimental results on fruit flies in the lab cannot be assumed to hold for wild flies, as biological complexity typically does not allow for context-independent or universal laws. Drawing on Woodward's (2003) manipulability account of causal generalizations, Waters however argues that experimenters need not assume complete invariance of causal principles.[22] Rather, scientists rely on what he calls "procedural knowledge" when stressing differences between experimental models and wildtypes. With this term, he stresses that the identified principles of inheritance in laboratory flies are seen as idealized because of the fixed laboratory environments and artificially induced regularity of cross-over rates. The importance of procedural knowledge does not make animal experimentation less valid, but it potentially makes results from animal research more context dependent. This also clarifies why it is not straightforward to integrate data on model organisms collected in different laboratory contexts, as this requires information about how the data were produced, including environmental conditions and protocols followed in different laboratories (Leonelli 2016).

Procedural knowledge requires awareness of external factors that may condition the outcome and potential for generalization to other contexts. Transparency about experimental protocols and better metadata about the conditions of data production are among the proposed solutions to address

---

[22] Woodward (2003) emphasizes the idea that causes are manipulable; that is, by intervening in a system, we can identify the causal relationships between variables.

the so-called replication crisis (Guttinger and Love 2019). Guttinger and Love, however, also stress the harder problem of "overgeneralization failure," that is, the risk of overlooking the causal relevance of parameters that are ignored or held fixed in a specific experimental situation without critical reflection. While translational failures are often attributed to differences between species, uncritical standardization of laboratory environments could be another source of failure. The problem of overgeneralization is hard to overcome because it results from a lack of knowledge about what variables can affect the phenomenon of interest.

Reconsidering laboratory standards is important for discussions of how "environmentally situated models" relate to the environmental conditions in the target settings (Ankeny et al. 2014). But it can also be important for reflections on what is assumed in the laboratory experiment itself. An important concern in behavioral neuroscience is that current interpretations may be confounded by a lack of attention to how artificial environments impact the behavior and brain activity in rodents. For example, animal modeling in research on dementia and Alzheimer's disease rely on an assumed causal relation between the failure to complete behavioral tasks and disease-induced memory loss. For such tasks, growing concerns relate to reflections on how animal experiments are often modeled according to optimal conditions for problem-solving in humans. For example, experiments are typically performed during daytime, even though rodents are nocturnal, because this is more convenient for human experimenters (Efstathiou 2019). Similarly, because laboratories are modeled according to human sensory systems, the reliance on smell in rodents and other animals (compared to vision) is often undervalued in cognitive neuroscience (Barwich 2023). The challenge is thus that "rodents do not see the world as we do" (Genzel 2021, p. 3). For instance, they do not naturally pay attention to differences in color in their environment, because they lack some of the color-related receptors, and some rodents (e.g., albino rats) have blurry vision. Meanwhile, they can easily be distracted by smells or sounds that are far below the levels detectable by human senses. Paradoxically, Genzel (2021) highlights that attempts to control for external factors can be counterproductive, because animals housed in environments with minimal noise may become more sensitive and less capable of ignoring sounds in behavioral tests. She therefore calls for more systematic exploration of how different environmental settings impact experimental results.

Some scholars have also highlighted how conventional laboratory housing restrict natural behaviors, such as nesting and burrowing, leading to stress-induced increases in morbidity and mortality in laboratory animals (Cait et al. 2022). Kirk and Ramsden (2018) argue that animal experiments must confront what they call an "ontological hybridity," where experimental designs not only privilege the human target of translation but also take animal needs and experiences into account. It is hoped that enrichment programs promoting the need for more naturalistic environments can improve both animal welfare and the validity of the experimental results (see also Davies et al. 2016). Whether caring for animals is compatible with objectivist ideals in science will be further discussed in Sections 4.3 and 4.4.

4 Animals as Patient Substitutes

4.1 Surrogate Models as Stand-ins for Patients

The special role of translational models as "substitutes" for human patients has implications for discussions about standardization and variation, as well as the relationship between humans and animals. Bolker's (2009) distinguishes surrogate models from exemplary models through differences in their scope of representation as well as their epistemic purposes. According to Bolker, *exemplary models* are material exemplars for generalizable traits. This description aligns with Ankeny and Leonelli's (2011; 2020) definition of model organisms as models representing a large class of organisms. In contrast to exemplary models, the aim of *surrogate models* is to serve as substitutes for specific human targets, such as specific human patients or patient groups in clinical trials. Surrogate models are important in drug development and regulatory approval. Successful preclinical trials on animals are generally considered a safety requirement before treatments are tested in human clinical trials, just like toxicity studies are first done in animals. The regulatory practices also highlight how the notion of "substitution" is a form of replacement, where the substitute is a proxy inferior to the original (Svendsen 2022, p. 11).

The scope of surrogate models is contingent on the perceived variation of human diseases and patients. The historical development of medicine has resulted in increasing numbers of disease categories and disease subtypes, as well as growing insights into the diversity of factors influencing disease development and treatment response. This complexity presents a challenge for animal-based translational research that is sometimes referred to as the problem of "extrapolation in heterogenous populations" (Steel 2008, p. 9). Hau (2008) elaborates on the problem by noting that: "As desirable as it often is to obtain results from a genetically defined and uniform animal model, the humans to whom the results are extrapolated are genetically highly variable, with cultural, dietary, and environmental differences" (p. 6). As mentioned in the introduction, proponents of precision medicine have recently called for new preclinical models that can better account for the biological variation between patients (Green et al. 2021; 2022; see also Section 6). The following sections will discuss examples of surrogate models taken to the extreme, via examples of "cancer avatars" and "patientized" models in biomedical research.

4.2 Mouse Avatars of Human Cancers

Difficulties of translating from standardized animal models to human clinical trials raise important questions about how similar the targets patients are. In oncology, translational challenges are increasingly attributed to the concerns about standardization practices, including the historical reliance on cancer mouse models based on standardized cancer cell lines. It is increasingly acknowledged that specific mutations can influence treatment response in cancer patients, but it is not possible to predict response directly from a genetic analysis. There is therefore a need for models that can allow for more stratified or even individualized "phenotypic testing."

PDXs, that is mouse models xenografted with tumor cells from diverse cancer patients, have been proposed as better translational models.[23] PDX models are sometimes developed to represent cancer subtypes, but they are also promoted as personalized models that recapitulate how "each individual cancer is characterized by patient-specific molecular events" (Izumchenko et al. 2017, p. 2595). The notion of "mouse avatar" is used informally by scientists to describe the vision of a "one patient paradigm" (Malaney et al. 2014), where each patient will have their own tumor grown in an in vivo system. Not surprisingly, this type of model has also gained attention from the popular press, describing these as "stand-ins for real people" (Perry 2013) and "the closest model to human cancer available without using humans themselves" (Schuellari 2015). PDX models thus raise philosophically intriguing questions about the relationship between animal model and human patient, as well as how personalized animal models impact evidence standards in medicine.

Figure 2 illustrates how PDX models can be used for patient-specific screening. A tumor sample is engrafted in an immunodeficient mouse. The tumor is grown to a certain size in the first host (F1), and then divided and expanded in a second generation of mice (F2). This process is called "passaging" and can be conducted in several generations of mice to expand on the tumor material. Meanwhile, targeted treatments options are identified based on omics analysis of a second biopsy or blood sample from the patient. The candidate

---

[23] For a comparison of the advantages and disadvantages of PDX models compared to syngeneic mouse models and xenografts based on standardized cancer cell lines, see Denayer et al. (2014) and Xu et al. (2019).

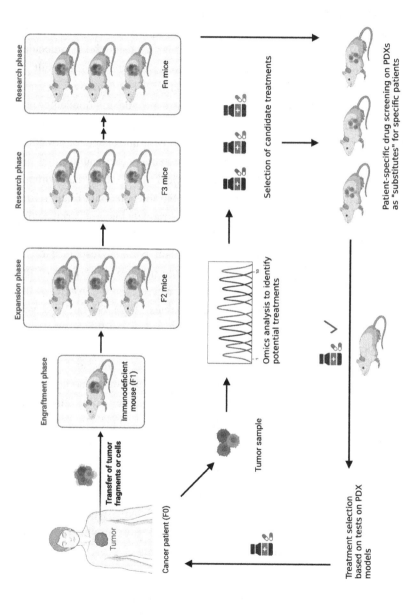

Figure 2 Illustration of the use of PDX models as "avatars" that serves as "substitutes" for specific patients. See text for details. The figure was created by the author with BioRender.com.

treatments can then be tested in the "avatar" models to guide selection of the most efficient treatment for the specific patient. Mouse avatars thus exemplify an extreme form of surrogate model, as they are not only *humanized* but also *personalized* to mimic patient-specific features.

Prospective observational studies comparing test results in PDX models and treatment outcomes in patients show promising prediction rates (reviewed in Green et al. 2021). But concerns have also been raised about molecular changes in the tumors of PDX models that are interpreted as the result of "mouse-specific tumor evolution" (Ben-David et al. 2017). Moreover, to grow human tumors in mice in the first place, the mouse must be immunocompromised, making these unsuitable for testing of immune therapies (Willyard 2018). Some researchers therefore emphasize the continued need for immunocompetent transplant models, even if they are syngeneic, meaning that the tumors are transplanted from genetically identical mice, rather than humans (Connolly et al. 2022). Others are optimistic about the potential of integrating all benefits in more advanced humanized mouse models that are "armed with human immune cells" (Nilsson et al. 2018; Mian et al. 2021), perhaps even mimicking the immune system in the individual patient (Jespersen et al. 2017). These attempts can be understood as the most extreme form of the "analog" modeling approach (Mazaratti 2007), where even the frontier of the species-specific immune system is pushed (Davies 2012). So far, however, mouse models with humanized immune systems are difficult and very resource-demanding to develop, offering another illustration of how criteria for organism choice may involve trade-offs in the epistemic and practical features (Dietrich et al. 2020). The example of mouse avatars also highlights how the translational potential of animal models has a temporal dimension. Compared to standardized "off-the-shelf" models, PDX models may be superior in identifying "the right drug for the right patient." But the right drug must also be identified "at the right time." Currently, the expansion phases illustrated in Figure 2 often exceed the time window of clinical decision-making, illustrating how the temporality of animal experimentation is not easily aligned with clinical needs (Green et al. 2021). This issue will be discussed further in Section 5.2. First, we examine additional ways in which surrogate models are constructed to stand in for human patients.

4.3 "Humanizing" and "Patientizing" Animal Models

Boundary work to tighten human–animal relations can take different shapes if substitution also requires that animal models enter the clinical space – as clinical models used for predictive purposes or as models that require mimicking of care practices in a hospital. Pig models are important models for this purpose due to their anatomical size, genetics, and physiological similarity to humans, as well as their high experimental accessibility (Lunney et al. 2021). The long history of pigs in agriculture means that translational researchers can draw on existing resources from agricultural science, such as knowledge on pig physiology and genetics, and standardized strains bred for indoor housing. Moreover, since millions of pigs are used each year for human consumption, the use of pigs in research are often perceived as less ethically problematic from a public perspective (Svendsen and Koch 2013; Svendsen 2022). But how are pig models simultaneously constructed as research subjects that are physically similar, yet morally distinct, from human patients?

Strategies to "humanize" and "dehumanize" pigs in transplantation research and surgical training offers intriguing insights to our ambiguous epistemic and emotional relationship to animals in translational research (Lowe 2022). "Humanizing" pig models involves transgenic modification of the pig models to overcome immunologically relevant differences between pigs and humans (Lowe 2022) as well as operational clinical and surgical procedures that resemble those involving humans patients (Jensen and Svendsen 2020). It is hoped that transplantation research using pig models can pave the way for optimized procedures in human transplantation, for example, to overcome current challenges in transplanting organs from so-called "marginal" donors. Yet, the pig models are also explicitly "dehumanized" through the different regulatory standards in experimentation and experimental treatments in pigs and humans. Ethnographic researchers also observe that such differences are enacted through different practices for handling bodily material following surgeries on humans and pigs. In the words of Jensen and Svendsen (2020), "the transplant research pig is not fully 'animal' but can certainly never be fully 'human'; it is appreciated because it spans the border zones of species and exceeds categories" (p. 124).

Pigs are also considered the favorite candidate as a resource for xenotransplantation in cases of donor organ shortage, because they are similar in physiology and organ size, and because species-barriers might be overcome with new gene editing technologies. Pig kidney and heart transplants have already been performed in studies on brain-dead humans (Reardon 2022), but these procedures are currently far from routine. Analyzing the history of xenotransplantation research, Lowe (2022) emphasizes that "however humanised [pigs] become, they must still remain pigs, as it is their non-human (and, indeed, non-primate) nature that makes them worthwhile candidates for this role" (Lowe 2022, p. 66). In the extraordinary medical spaces where the spaces of the laboratory and the clinic overlap, pigs take on roles as a kind of liminal existence that is "near" but never fully human (Svendsen 2022; see also Mol et al. 2010).

Another important place where pigs enter medicine is in neonatology, as documented by Dam and colleagues' ethnographic research on an interdisciplinary collaboration between a neonatal clinic and an animal laboratory developing a "preterm pig model" (Sangild et al. 2014; Dam et al. 2017; 2018). This model is used to study the effects of nutritional interventions on the gastrointestinal system and brain development among prematurely born infants. To serve this purpose, piglets are delivered by C-section at a developmental timeline corresponding to body functions of infants born at 27 weeks of gestation. In this context, however, it is not sufficient that the piglets are physiologically "human-like." They must also be sufficiently "patient-like" for clinicians to recognize their value as translational models that can guide treatment decisions in clinical neonatal care. Dam and Svendsen (2018) coin the term "patientized models" to capture how the preterm piglets are treated like human infants in the neonatal clinic, where almost everything will be done to increase the survival chances of the preterm infants. Researchers are even instructed to "treat [piglet] like it was your own son" (quote from a PI in Dam and Svendsen 2018, p. 358). This involves conduction of medical interventions that are far beyond what is typical in animal experiments, such as CPR procedures, continuous oxygen supply, and meticulous attention to the piglets' healthcare needs. Researchers also engage in emotional work, for example, by calming down a distressed piglet by talking and singling in a calming voice. Dam and colleagues argue that by caring for piglets in ways like they would with a human infant, divides are straddled between the animal and the human. Because of this "contamination" of human–animal relations, preterm piglet models occupy a morally ambiguous space between human patients and "mere" animal models (Dam and Svendsen 2018; Dam et al. 2018).

Importantly, however, the construction of an animal–infant–patient hybrid does not dissolve the moral hierarchy between piglet and human infant. Moral boundaries are redrawn as killing piglets is a requirement for turning experimental results into translational research data. As also observed by Sharp (2013), such practices reveal how translational animal models are "simultaneously expandable and extraordinarily valuable" (p. 46). Similarly, although Dam and colleagues observe how animal researchers are exceptionally allowed to bring the pigs into the hospital to use the hospital's MR-scanner, distinctions are upheld as the pigs can only enter through the hospital's back door (Dam et al. 2018). The "plasticity" of piglet preterm models to bridge the divides between the laboratory and the clinic, and between animals and humans, also involves the flexibility of human researchers to continuously relate to and distance themselves from the animal model (Dam et al. 2020). This raises broader questions about the compatibility of emotional work and objectivity in biomedical science.

4.4 Caring for Animals to Study Human Disease

Preclinical and clinical research practices are often characterized by positivist scientific norms implying that research should follow standardized methods and procedures to eliminate subjective experiences, emotions, and opinions from influencing the scientific process. Drawing on Levinas' concept of "technologies of effacement," Efstathiou (2019) argues that animal research is structured around practices that deliberately condition and limit emotional encounters between humans and animals in the lab. These include the reliance on specific protective garments and equipment, labelling techniques, experimental protocols, and the standardized architectures and procedures for entering and exiting animal labs. Such practices serve important epistemic purposes to control variables, avoid contamination via hygiene procedures, and ensure consistent labelling, and so on, which again improve repeatability and reproducibility of results. However, as "technologies of effacement," these procedures also prevent researchers from facing animals as morally significant beings (Efstathiou 2019). It is not uncommon that researchers report on ambiguity in their relations to animal models (Svendsen and Koch 2013; Nelson 2018, pp. 8–9), which calls for further philosophical studies of how animal research requires both epistemic and emotional work in relating to and distancing ourselves from experimental animals. Can objectivist norms of quantitative science be aligned with ideographic explanations based on subjective relational and emotional experiences of animal behavior? These questions will be unpacked through additional examples.

Kirk and Ramsden (2018) provide a fascinating historical analysis of how this question has played out in comparative psychobiology, developed by Howard Liddell (1985–1962) and colleagues in the period from 1923 to 1962. At the so-called Behavior Farm, Liddell and colleagues studied how animals (primarily sheep and goats) respond to trauma over longer time periods. In this process, Liddell observed how relational bonds of intimacy, trust, and collaboration formed between animal subject and human investigator, analogous to the relationship between patient and psychotherapist (Liddell 1942). Liddell's work exemplifies what Kirk and Ramsden interpret as a productive tension between "the desire for objective quantified knowledge and the intimated knowledge (or 'case history') of the individual animal" (Kirk and Ramsden 2018, p. 18). Concerns were raised about how the experimenter's relationship to animal research subjects could confound results or entail a problematic anthropomorphizing of animals. Liddell and colleagues, in contrast, argued that the criticism was guilty of human exceptionalism and called for greater acknowledgment of homologous behaviors and emotions in human and non-human animals. From this perspective, the relatedness in human–animal behaviors and interactions is not reducible to a mere analogy but is justified by conserved psychobiological reactions to trauma. In their perspective, the shared evolutionary history makes it possible for human experimenters to understand animal behavior.[24]

Caring relations between human experimenter and animals thus have a contested status, if not simply considered irrelevant for or in opposition to proper scientific practice. Friese et al. (2019) observe that it is common to view caring for animals as something that separates technicians and animal trainers from scientists. In other words, animal husbandry (the work involved in feeding, housing, handling, and reproducing laboratory animals) and basic handling of animals is often considered as "extra-scientific concern that animal technicians and veterinarians are responsible for, as opposed to scientists themselves" (p. 2043). Yet, Friese and colleague argue that this view is not in alignment with actual scientific practice, as caring of animals is often considered as a precondition for good data and robust translational outcomes (Friese 2013; Davies et al. 2016: Friese et al. 2019). Animal welfare is therefore not only an ethical concern but also a historical and epistemic issue concerning the validity of animal models that must also encompass behavioral and emotional traits. Particularly important in these debates are concerns about the possibility of translating results from experimental studies if these include procedures that stress the animals (Kirk 2014; see also Nelson 2018, pp. 8–9). Historical debates on the 3R principles to replace, reduce, and refine animal models (see in Section 6) also revolve around the relationship between hard science and humanistic values (Kirk 2018). Yet, as Efstathiou (2019) remarks: "Nowhere in these guidelines are the humans' encounters with animals in research considered ethically significant in themselves" (p. 144). Rather, the ethical and emotional tensions felt by researchers typically stay hidden in the animal laboratory. This topic thus adds to the list of philosophical questions on animal models that may require methodologies beyond content analysis to uncover and which have not yet received much philosophical attention.

5 Beyond Disease Representation

Most of the literature on models in the philosophy of science focuses on representational relations between models and targets. But the materiality and status of animal organisms as living beings also extend the philosophical questions beyond purely representational issues. This section first examines the instrumental roles of animals in biomedicine, showing how other epistemic features than

---

[24] Similar questions are discussed in contemporary research on pain and pain-related behaviors in humans and animals (see Section 6.1).

representational matching matter for organism choice (Section 5.1). Two such features include the temporality of model development (Section 5.2) and the size of the animal or animal part (Section 5.3). Finally, we examine the role of animal models as collaborative and material recourses (Section 5.4).

5.1 Instrumental Roles of Animals in Biomedicine

In a paper entitled "From replica to instruments: animal models in biomedical research," Germain (2014) argues that the role of animals as *biomedical instruments* is more prevalent in biomedical research than typically recognized by philosophers of science. Instrument in this context means a device or diagnostic tool that links a causal input to an observable signal. Inclusion of the instrumental roles of animals in the philosophical discussion is important to uncover how some animal models are not only used to understand human diseases, but also as vehicles for diagnostic predictions. To serve this role, strong representational similarity between model and target may be neither necessary nor sufficient, as discussed in the following.

Interesting historical examples of the instrumental use of animals includes testing for pregnancy and cancer via injection of human urine in animals sensitive to the "pregnancy hormone" gonadotrophin. It the late 1920s, researchers discovered that injection of urine from pregnant women in juvenile mice led to fast maturation of ovarian follicles and observable dark spots on these. This test, also known as the Ascheim-Zondek (A-Z) reaction test, was implemented as a diagnostic tool in Britain in the 1930s (Germain 2014; Olszynko-Gryn 2014). Other animals used for similar procedures were rats, rabbits, and later also frogs (Olszynko-Gryn 2013; 2014). The latter had the advantage that the animal did not have to be killed and dissected to provide an observable signal, because the physiological response to human gonadotrophin was production of significantly larger eggs. While the ability of some animals to play this role is based on the evolutionary conservation of reproduction-related hormone signaling pathways, Germain (2014) stresses that the inferences drawn from the animals are not dependent on a representational similarity between the physiological output signal in the animal (maturation of ovarian follicles or larger eggs) and the human condition of interest (pregnancy). Rather, what matters is whether the animal test provides a measurable and reproducible physiological response of medical relevance.

As chemical home pregnancy tests became available, this diagnostic function of animals for pregnancy testing became obsolete (Leavitt 2006). However, the A-Z reaction test also served another – and more important – biomedical role as a diagnostic test for hormonal deficiencies associated with abnormal placental activity and related pathologies. Olszynko-Gryn (2014) shows how historical debates on the interpretation of the A-Z test led to further refinement of the test in mice as a detector of early development of placental cancer, increased risk of miscarriage, and infertility. This involved calibration of testing results to reflect a graded series of reactions reflecting the spectrum from very low to very high endocrine levels, thus distinguishing "true pregnancy" from pathological hormonal states (Olszynko-Gryn 2014, p. 242). Again, what matters is not so much *what* is represented but whether physiological output signals have predictive validity for specific purposes (e.g., prognostics or prediction of treatment efficacy).

More recently, the exploration of simple animal models in toxicology also challenges the view that good translational models are those that maximally represent human physiology. Mice and rats have traditionally been used to identify adverse effects of chemical compounds in medicine, industry, agriculture, and consumer products. Yet, the production of evidence from studies on mice and rats is currently lacking behind the industrial production of new chemicals (Carusi, forthcoming). This is especially the case for endocrine disrupting chemicals which often do not cause acute toxicity but can impact fertility as well as cause developmental defects in the next generation. One way to address this challenge is to utilize alternative – and simpler – animal models that are faster to develop. Alternative models include small invertebrate models, such as zebrafish and zebrafish larvae, and invertebrates, such as snails or roundworms (Morthorst et al. 2023; Ramhøj et al. 2023). Researchers can for instance exploit how the natural process of sex change in zebrafish can be altered through environmental exposure to sex hormones. Although the zebrafish's capacity of sex change is very dissimilar to human physiology, their sensitivity and direct responsiveness to endocrine disruptors can make zebrafish superior for predictive purposes, compared to a more "representationally realistic" model. While it should be acknowledged that the utility of these "simpler" models is based on conserved endocrine signaling pathways in zebrafish and humans, the output signal (e.g., sex changes) need not represent the human condition to provide medically relevant results.

A final, and quite intriguing, example of animals as detection devices is the reliance on the strong sense of smell in some species. Just like dogs can detect toxic gasses in mines or drugs in luggage, sniffing animals can be used to detect infectious diseases in human stool, urine, sputum, skin, or breath, because many microorganisms produce specific and identifiable odors. While some of these are detectable by humans, scent detection in sniffing animals is estimated to be 10,000–100,000 times stronger than human acuity (Cambau and Poljak 2020). Examples include the use of rats to detect tuberculosis and reliance on dogs to detect bacteria species associated with bowel infections. Since humans rely on the enhanced senses of animals to smell substances at concentrations below what is possible for humans, it could be argued that interpreting the role of sniffing animals as a detection device is misleading. Yet, just like the representational role of animals can be improved via human-animal relationships (Section 4.4), the role of animals as detection devices need not imply a reduction of animals to mere tools. Rather, in this case, it could be argued that human–animal relations are essential to the training of sniffing animals and thus another example where emotional relations not only threaten but also *constitute* knowledge practices.

It should also be noted that the use of animals as diagnostic tools or detection devices does not always involve the whole animal. For example, horseshoe crabs play an extremely important role in the development of vaccines and other injection-based treatments, but this only involves horseshoe crabs as blood donors. The blood of horseshoe crabs has exceptional antibacterial properties and contains a unique clotting agent (limulus amebocyte lysate (LAL)) that coagulates around toxic Gram-negative bacteria (Krisfalusi-Gannon et al. 2018). Because horseshoe crabs are the only natural source of LAL, the medical industry heavily relies on their blue blood to check for bacterial contamination of vaccines and other products.[25] While the example of horseshoe crabs, like the A-Z reaction test, is a clear example of an instrumental use of animals in medicine, other cases are less clear-cut. Surrogate models often combine the two functions of i) models representing selected features of a medical condition of interest, and ii) *diagnostic tools* for practical purposes (prediction of treatment response).

An example of a less clear-cut example is the PDX cancer model discussed in Section 4.2. These can serve important roles as models in preclinical research, because xenotransplantation of human tumors is intended to better recapitulate what is distinctive of human cancers. Mouse avatars can, however, also take on the role as a diagnostic tool for clinical decision-making. This shows that the distinction between the use of animals as models and as diagnostic tools is not an inherent feature of the animal. The same animal model can be used as a model or an instrument, depending on the experimental context (Germain 2014; Olszynko-Gryn 2014). This point is also illustrated in the following section with the development of smaller "avatar" models, such as zebrafish

---

[25] The extensive use of horseshoe crabs by the medical industry has raised concerns about exploitation, disruption of ecosystem balance, and risk of species extinction (CBS News 2020). Researchers currently attempt to develop synthetic alternatives to the use of horseshoe crab blood for endotoxin detection (Maloney et al. 2018), but no alternatives have been implemented yet.

and fruit flies, where the instrumental function of fast diagnostic testing becomes even more salient.

5.2 The Temporality of Translational Models

Although temporality is not listed as one of the 20 criteria for model choice in Table 1, temporal aspects underlie several practical criteria on the list, including "ease of supply," "tractability," and "viability and durability" (Dietrich et al. 2020). A short generation time can sometimes be more important than close physiological similarity and is important for understanding why organisms such as fruit flies and zebrafish have become so widespread as models in biomedical research. Choosing organisms with a specific temporality of life cycles is also important for modeling *temporal* disease-related processes. By choosing *C. elegans* as a model for development or aging or age-related diseases, scientists can "speed up" the aging process and study the molecular and phenotypic changes over shorter periods. For surrogate models, however, temporality becomes a factor not only for the timeframe of laboratory work but also something that needs to be aligned with *clinical* temporalities and demands. As seen in Section 4.3, the "preterm piglet model" must not only be temporally matched with prematurely born infants through scheduled C-sections but also through the temporalities of care practices and medical procedures to resemble the human clinical context (Dam and Svendsen 2018; see also Lowe et al. 2020)

Temporality is particularly pressing for organism choice when animal models are used as *diagnostic tools* for decision-making in real time. As indicated in Section 4.2, the vision of patient-specific drug screening via "cancer avatars" requires that the animal model is temporally aligned with, or ideally ahead of, the human patient. However, developing PDX models within the clinically meaningful time window for treatment decisions is currently a major barrier to translation because it often takes longer to develop and passage tumor materials in PDX models than patients can wait for treatment decisions to be taken (Xu et al. 2019). Strategies to address this temporal challenge include systematic improvement of experimental procedures as well as initiatives to develop so-called "living biobanks" of cancer tissue cultures, where cryopreserved samples from patients with similar cancer types can be used for drug screening for individual treatment decisions (Green et al. 2021). The latter strategy is, however, a step away from patient-specific models and towards a more stratified approach, and such biobanks are still at early stages of development.

Another philosophically intriguing option is to speed up translation by choosing smaller avatar models. *Zebrafish xenografts* present an interesting way of transforming a traditional model organism into a personalized surrogate model with a narrow representational scope. These can either be developed by implementation of a human oncogene into a plasmid vector or by microinjection of single-cell suspensions of a patient-derived tumor into larvae or adult zebrafish. This procedure has shown some promising (although still preliminary) results for the prediction of chemotherapy sensitivity in patients with colon cancer and leukemia (Fazio et al. 2020). Choosing zebrafish speeds up the translational process of drug testing, from weeks or months for mouse PDXs to days in the case of zebrafish larvae, and it also allows for much higher drug screening throughput to validate test results. Even smaller – and faster – candidates for cancer avatars are genetically engineered *fruit fly models*. "Fly avatars" are transgenic fruit flies with altered orthologs corresponding to patient-specific mutations. The phenotypic readout of this model system is reduced lethality when specific drugs are combined with the fly's food. With fly avatars, it is possible to test hundreds of drugs and drug combinations via a robotics-based screening tool. For example, a pioneering study conducted in 2019 used 400,000 fruit flies to test a library of 1500 drugs and drug combinations, as a proof-of-principle to guide treatment selection for a single patient with advanced colon cancer (Bangi et al. 2019; Cagan et al. 2019; Choutka et al. 2022).

Smaller personalized models can provide faster test results, but the smaller size also comes with some trade-offs. Not all cancers or cancer-related features can be modeled in small organisms. For example, there is no direct transfer of human material to a "fly avatar," and these models are primarily suited for colon cancer drug screens. Similarly, only a small number of human cells can be grown in a zebrafish xenograft, which makes these models limited for studying tumor dynamics and development of treatment resistance over time (Zanella et al. 2022). Rather than replacing mouse models, the small avatars may therefore be useful as part of a combinatorial approach, where zebrafish or fruit flies can offer fast high-throughput results to guide the selection of treatments to be tested further in more resource-demanding models.

The temporality of model development has not yet received much attention from philosophers of science, perhaps because temporality is primarily considered a practical constraint and not an epistemic issue. However, as translational models enter clinical spaces, temporal matching of model and target can be as important as representational features. Moreover, attention to the temporality of models can also inform about the perceived variation in and temporality of the disease itself. One important argument for using faster and simpler animal model for cancer drug screening is that cancer is increasingly considered as a fast-moving (i.e., evolving) target that may require different combinations of drugs at different times. The celebrated model virtues are thus linked to fundamental questions about what constitutes the most salient features of the diseases studied.

5.3 Estimating Drug Dosage and Toxicity: Scaling Problems and Other Challenges

Animals are not only used to develop and select effective treatments for human patients but also to estimate the relevant *drug dosages* and test for drug-induced toxicity. Animals with similar physiology to humans (mice, rats, and non-human primates) can help researchers understand how drugs are metabolized, distributed, and excreted from the body and are also used to estimate what drug dosage are safe for human consumption. For this purpose, size matters. Yet, the scientific problem of spatial scalability between animal models and humans in drug dosage estimation has, to my knowledge, not yet received much attention from philosophers of science.

Drug dosage in humans cannot be extrapolated linearly with body size in animal models because of allosteric scaling relations. The metabolic rate of small animals, such as mice, is significantly higher than large animals, because the density of capillaries and the heart rate increase nonlinearly as body weight decreases. As a result, small animals have significantly higher heart rates, respiration, and food intake than larger mammals (Schmidt-Nielsen 1984; Hau 2008). An example often found in physiology textbooks illustrates this well, although the context is animal behavioral research. In the 1960s, the interest in elephants in zoos and circuses created a need for studying, under controlled conditions, how the rageful and often destructive behavior of male elephants during mating season could be managed in captivity. Applying a conceptual modeling approach (Section 2.1), scientists hypothesized that similar behavior could be induced via the psychedelic drug, lysergic acid diethylamide (LSD), whose effects were at that time primarily known in humans. Unfortunately, the scientists failed to properly account for the differences in metabolic rates of humans and elephants, leading to a fatal overdose in the elephant Tusco, as described in the resulting publication in *Science* (West et al. 1962; see also West 2017). The study was criticized for several reasons, one of them being that allometric scaling laws were formulated already in the 1930s, denoting how metabolic rates scale nonlinearly with body mass (Kleiber 1932; Marcus 2016). The metabolic rate (M) is defined as the oxygen consumption per body weight per hour, and the relation between the metabolic rate and body weight (BW) scales as follows:

$$M = 3.8 \times BW^{-0.25}$$

To extrapolate experimentally defined drug doses from one animal to another animal with different body size, the following equation is often used as guidance:

$$Dose_1 = Dose_2 \times BW_1^{-0.25}/BW_2^{-0.25}$$

Because drug responses can vary significantly between and even within species (and with environmental conditions), different conversion factors have been developed for different animal models, and safety factors are often applied (Nair and Jacob 2016). But just like Tusco was overdosed because of lacking attention to allometric scaling, the same would happen to humans if dosages are not adjusted to differences in metabolic rates of mice, rats, and humans.

Animal research also informs regulatory practices on threshold levels for chemical substances in medicine, processed food, and so on. Thresholds of toxicological concern are extrapolated from the observed NOAEL (No Observed Adverse Effect Level) in studies on mice or rats, but these results are divided by a safety factor to account for differences between animal studies and human physiology, and often a further safety factor to account for differences between humans. Whether this approach provides sufficient safety measures has, however, been debated, especially if test results are not only extrapolated across species but also across structurally similar chemical compounds (Bschir 2017).

Scaling laws should generally be used with caution, as it is unclear to what extent quantitative safety estimates can account for *qualitative differences* between specifies (LaFollette and Shanks 1995). Different animals not only metabolize drugs at different rates and but to different degrees and with different physiological responses. For example, drugs that target the human heart rhythm do not have the same effects in mice (Dutch Foundation for Biosciences and Society 2020, p. 14). New drugs are therefore commonly tested in different types of in vitro and in vivo systems. Moreover, clinical (phase I) trials involving a small group of (healthy) human participants are used to evaluate the safety of new drugs before these are approved for larger clinical trials. These trials involve carefully monitoring participants' responses to different doses of the drug and adjusting these according to observed outcomes.

Why are animal models not sufficient to guarantee patient safety in drug testing? Some substances have turned out be toxic for humans but not in animals – and vice versa. An often-mentioned example illustrating this problem is the thalidomide scandal in the late 1950s and early 1960s. Following positive results in toxicity testing on rodents, thalidomide was misleadingly marketed as safe for humans, including treatment of morning sickness and other types of discomfort in pregnant women. However, marketing of the drug led to more than 10,000 several birth defects in infants worldwide (LaFollette and Shanks 1993). It would be misleading to attribute the full scale of the tragedy to the failure of animal experiments, as the thalidomide case is also a tragic story about the consequences of insufficient standards for post-marketing drug surveillance. But the case does raise the question if better animal experiments could have prevented the tragedy. The thalidomide scandal led to changes in drug authorization procedures, with new regulations requiring testing also for teratogenicity (effects on developing embryos) in different animal species (Swaters et al. 2022). In this case, however, subsequent testing of teratogenicity in the 1970s using different species (including dogs, hamsters, primates, cats, guineapigs, ferrets, and pigs) failed to reveal statistically significant results comparable to the developmental defects observed in humans (Lafollette and Shanks 1995). The thalidomide case and other historical examples thus raise concerns that animals may be sacrificed to merely produce a minimal or even false sense of safety (Swaters et al. 2022).

Another example underscoring this concern is the translational failure of the drug called TGN1412, a genetically engineered antibody intended as a treatment against some forms of leukemia and rheumatoid arthritis (Striedter 2022, pp. 11–12). Based on preclinical experiments on rats and macaque monkeys, tolerable treatment doses were extrapolated to healthy human subjects in a small phase-I trial. However, all six patients had severe reactions to the drug and were transferred to intensive care units, some with multiple organ failure. Later studies revealed differences in immune responses between rats, macaque monkeys, and humans due to molecular differences in T-cells. As lessons from the trial, Striedter (2022) highlights not only the dangers of extrapolating from animal models to humans but also the need for more advanced in vitro experiments based on human cells or tissues.

The call for alternative methods in drug development and drug approval is also motivated by the opposite concern – that some compounds have adverse effects in animals but not in humans. As most dog owners know, chocolate ingestion can lead to significant toxic effects and illness in dogs. Chocolate contains theobromine (and often also caffeine), which dogs – unlike humans – cannot easily metabolize. Because preclinical animal models serve as "gatekeepers" for first-in-human clinical trials, such metabolic differences could lead to unfounded rejection of potentially useful treatments for humans. Indeed, it has been estimated that paracetamol – one of the most used painkillers – would not have made it to clinical trials if first tested in dogs. Recent reviews of outcomes of human-directed animal experimentation also suggest that translational success rates are highly unpredictable (Leenaars et al. 2019). Yet, as further discussed in Sections 5.4 and 6, animal models are not easily replaced with alternative methods. One reason is that animal models serve multiple socio-epistemic functions in research communities (Ankeny and Leonelli 2016; Lohse 2021), and translational success is not easily reduced to concordance rates between animal model and human target (as also acknowledged by Leenaars et al. 2019).

5.4 Animals as Collaborative and Material Resources

Davies (2012) suggests that animal models are not only "epistemic things" (Rheinberger 1997) but also "collaborative things" that offer open-ended possibilities for interdisciplinary encounters and synergies. Already Krogh (1929) stressed the importance of such collaborations in highlighting the benefits of insights from zoology for animal experimentation in human physiology and medicine.[26] Similarly, García-Sancho and Lowe (2023) unpack how human genomics historically depended on extensive collaborations between research communities focused on human and animal genomics. The collaborative value of animal models is also instrumental in coordinating interactions and exchange of expertise across the laboratory and the clinic (Sharp 2019). Jensen and Svendsen (2020) contend that the development of pig models for surgical training and transplantation depends on and opens for "collaborative intimacies" between animal researchers and medical professionals. Similarly, "avatar models" for patient-specific drug screening currently reshape institutional boundaries between laboratory research and the clinic through continuous exchanges of bodily material and test results for patient management in real time (Green et al. 2021).

The collaborative function of animal models is also explicit in the central role of repositories in model organism research, such as gene ontologies and stock collections of animal strains (Ankeny and Leonelli 2020). Model organisms bring together different communities that agree on practices for "storing, maintaining, and disseminating stocks on demand" (p. 37). Such exchanges also go beyond academic research because animal models (such as JAX mice) are also material resources for commercial investment (Rader 2004). Animal models can thus take on roles as living commodities that can be patented, traded, and co-developed through complex social relations that greatly influence what types of research can be done.

---

[26] Krogh founded a "Zoophysiological Laboratory" in Copenhagen in 1910, which became an important venue for the development of what is now known as comparative physiology (for details, see Schmidt-Nielsen 1995/2019). The term "zoophysiology" (zoofysiologi) is still widely used in Denmark.

The role of animals as material resources for commercial gain and human experimentation is not uncontroversial. An intriguing example that sparked public debates is the so-called EMOUSE (or earmouse), a nude mouse growing a structure resembling a human ear on its back. A picture of the strange-looking mouse was released around the same time as the publication of the corresponding scientific study on tissue engineering (Cao et al. 1997). The picture quickly spread in news media worldwide and raised ethical concerns about animal welfare, patient safety, as well as broader implications of gene technologies. The earmouse was, however, not an example of mouse genetically manipulated to grow a human tissue. Rather, the nude mouse was developed as an immuno-compromised "host" to explore the feasibility of transplanting a tissue-engineered cartilage (based on polymers and cow cartilage cells) to a living organism without being rejected.[27] Still, the earmouse may be a precursor for more extensive uses of animals as "livestock hosts." With recent developments in stem cell technologies and CRISPR-Cas9, the possibilities for development and maintenance of human organs for translation are increasing (Morata Tarifa et al. 2020). New technological possibilities therefore reignite debates about the moral risk of crossing human–animal boundaries in chimeras, about patient safety, as well as the instrumental uses of animals as living resources for biomedical consumption and commercial gain. This brings us to the final section discussing the ambiguous moral relationships to animal models and the possibilities for replacing them with animal-free methods.

6 The Status and Future of Animal Models

Although animal models are selected and engineered to fit human biomedical needs, practices of animal modeling reflect back on our understanding of human disease and nature – including our capacity to relate, physically and emotionally, to other animals. As Rader puts it, the history of animal models in medicine encourages us "to engage with the questions of animal and human integrity that now define biomedicine and, in the process, define us" (Rader 2004, p. 268). The use of animals to learn about human physiology and disease goes back to ancient Greece, and comparative dissections and experiments on living animals are central pillars in the history of experimental studies in physiology and medicine (Ericsson et al. 2013). In this history, there is a persistent tension in the relatedness of human and non-human animals and the moral devaluation of animals as simple means to improve human health. Many breakthroughs in the history of medicine are based on animal suffering,

---

[27] The synthetic scaffold was shaped as a human ear, because this structure is difficult to reconstruct via plastic surgery (e.g., after injuries).

exposing an uncomfortable ambiguity in our appreciation of animals and instrumental uses of them. Although the ethical standards of animal experiments have improved substantially, moral ambiguities and conflicts remain. In this final section, we examine some of these and reflect on the future of animal models.

6.1 Animals and Us

The use of animals in biomedical research is surrounded by epistemic uncertainty and ethical conflicts. Rader's (2004) book on the making of mouse models contains intriguing historical images expressing the ambiguous relations between humans and animals. They depict relations ranging from fear and hate towards mice as unwanted inhabitants of human facilities, to emotional relations when mice take on roles as pets, and to gratitude and embarrassment about their sacrifices for human medicine. In the words of Rader, these images "remain powerful as much for their ability to bring us together under an umbrella of common humanity served by these animals, as to tear us apart in periodic waves of social and ethical conflict over the meaning of their creation and use" (Rader 2004, p. 264). Similarly, as Svendsen (2022) beautifully illustrates in her book *Near Human*, practices of substitution in the bio-clinical border zone of translational research and modern society involve ambiguities concerning what lives are worth saving. Animal models are considered extremely valuable and worthy of care, but they must – as human proxies – be used and sacrificed to produce biomedical data (Sharp 2019). Fundamentally, our ambiguous relationship with animals in science therefore also brings to question what it means to be human and how different humans and other animals really are (Efstathiou 2019; Ramsey 2013; 2023).

Practices of animal modeling also expose how not all animals are considered morally equal. The more animals resemble humans, the more ethically problematic we often consider their use as animal models. But how is this moral ranking justified and is it consistent? The notion of the "socio-zoological scale" is often used to describe how we tend to view animals morally differently, depending not only on zoological classification but also on our social (historical and cultural) relationship with particular species (Arluke and Sanders 1996). As discussed in the cases of mouse and pig models, their widespread use has also been facilitated by cultural beliefs that experimenting on these animals is less problematic than animals we tend to emotionally relate to as pets. But to what extent are such practices compatible with evidence-based regulation of animal research, and on what scientific basis do we evaluate which animals are capable of feeling pain and complex emotions? The socio-zoological scale has been criticized for being grounded in speciesism and human exceptionalism (Gruen 2003/2017; Jones 2022). While there is consensus in regulatory practices that scientists should choose "lower" animals with simpler physiology or more limited cognitive capacities, when possible (see the following section), determining what animals count as morally acceptable experimental models for different purposes is a difficult question.

The scope of animals considered capable of experiencing pain and anxiety has historically expanded through insights from biological research on animal sentience and behavior (Jones 2022; Kiani et al. 2022). Epistemic and ethical questions are closely intertwined in such discussions. The historical debates on whether fish are capable of conscious experiences of pain illustrate this well. Depending on theoretical standpoints and views on operationalization of pain in experiments, data on behavioral changes after acid injections or similar stimuli have been interpreted differently. Some argued that assessment of pain experiences in non-human animals should be based on our best available neurophysiological knowledge of pain in humans, and that a lack of conscious experiences of pain in fish can be inferred from the lack of analogous neurological and brain structures (Key 2015; 2016). From this perspective, interpreting behavioral reactions to stimuli as pain, instead of mere nociception, amounts to anthropomorphizing animal behaviors. Others, in contrast, argued that rejecting the possibility of pain experience in fish on this ground reflects a problematic anthropocentric starting point in human neurology that fails to realize how similar cognitive capacities can result from evolutionarily contingent neurological traits (Sneddon 2015; Sneddon and Leach 2016). Both accounts thus criticize the other camp for basing inferences on the case of humans. While the lack of a common semantic language marks a critical difference between studies of pain in humans and animals, philosophical problems in behavioral psychology and animal research often overlap and revolve around the negotiation of what unites and differentiates human and non-human experiences (Godfrey-Smith 2020).

Today, there is widespread consensus that fish can pass behavioral tests that are accepted as evidence of sentience in other animals, suggesting that they can feel some kind of pain and discomfort (Jones 2022). Indeed, fish are increasingly granted the same regulatory protection as other vertebrates. But another contested moral and regulatory boundary remains between vertebrate and invertebrate animal models. An EU Directive of January 1, 2013, gave cephalopods (cuttlefish, nautilus, octopus, and squids) the same legal status as vertebrate models, following research demonstrating sentience and cognitive capacities comparable to many vertebrates (Smith et al. 2013). However, the same rights do currently not apply to cephalopods in the US

(Preston 2022). Moreover, other invertebrates are not currently protected by regulations of animal experimentation or even reported in the total count of animals used in translational research. Research on crustaceans and insects, however, indicates the uncomfortable possibility that the scope of sentient animals that can feel discomfort and pain is much greater than previously thought (Sneddon 2015; Godfrey-Smith 2020; Jones 2022; Veit 2022). The difficulty of drawing sharp boundaries is also seen in shifting regulatory practices for how to handle embryonic or larvae stages of vertebrates (e.g., zebrafish) in experiments.

Capacities that unite humans and non-human animals are simultaneously paving the way for translational inferences and giving rise to ethical concerns and conflicts. The use of animals in translational research is typically justified with reference to the benefits for medical research and human health. As examples in and beyond this Element illustrate, animal models have led to important insights in medicine. But how significant the utility of animals models is for medicine is a contested issue (LaFollette and Shanks 1993; 1995). The status of animal models as a "gold standard" of preclinical research and gatekeeper for first-in-human trial is being questioned (Thompson 2013; Swaters et al. 2022). We therefore next turn to a brief examination of ethical principles to improve animal welfare in translational research as well as possible animal-free methods.

6.2 The 3R Principles

Translational challenges, as well as concerns about animal welfare, have motivated calls for institutional and regulatory changes to substitute animal models with animal-free methods. The 3R principles, which stand for Replacement, Reduction, and Refinement, were already introduced in the 1950s by British scientists Russell and Burch. Their seminal book *The Principles of Humane Experimental Technique* (1959) was a response to growing concerns about the welfare of animals used in research and considerations about how to reduce animal use while still advancing scientific knowledge (Kirk 2018). The principle of *Replacement* states that non-animal methods must be used when possible. This principle recognizes that some studies can be conducted without animals, for example, by experimenting on human cells. The principle of *Reduction* states that experiments should include as few animals as possible. The call for reduction encourages scientists to consider whether the number of animals used in research could be reduced without compromising the scientific validity of the study. Finally, the principle of *Refinement* states that animal experiments should be refined to improve animal welfare. This principle recognizes that some animal studies are still necessary but that efforts must be made to reduce pain and distress, for example, by improvements to experimental protocols and housing conditions.

An example of the 3R principles at work is the attempt to replace and reduce rodent models in toxicology testing. A growing number of researchers are engaged in an *adverse outcome pathways networks*, which is a framework for gathering and organizing data an information about adverse outcomes of treatments and chemical compounds (Ankley et al. 2010; Carusi et al. 2022a; 2022b). As part of this work, different types of evidence (e.g., statistical and mechanistic) from different studies are combined and compared in order to identify correspondences and knowledge gaps. Moreover the predictive validity of possible alternative models is compared to standard rodent models. As mentioned, alternative models can include small invertebrate models, such as zebrafish and zebrafish larvae, and invertebrates, such as snails or roundworms (Morthorst et al. 2023; Ramhøj et al. 2023). But alternative models also include new approach methods (NAMs) such as in vitro models based on human cells, computer simulations as well as synthetic materials and artificial "human-like" surgical models for diagnostic testing and medical training (Wittwehr et al. 2017; Carusi et al. 2022a; 2022b; Swaters et al. 2022).

The focus on the 3R principles has intensified in the wake of the so-called replication crisis, exposing difficulties of reproducing results in animal studies in other laboratories or in first-in-human-trials (Frommlett et al. 2021; Striedter 2022). A systematic review of reported concordance rates in animal to human translation found a wide range of translational success rates (between 0–100 percent), with high variability both within and between study types and animal models, suggesting that the reliability of many animal models is largely unpredictable (Leenaars et al. 2019). Similarly, a report developed by the Dutch Foundation for Bioscience and Society estimates that "90% of the promising drugs that are tested for the first time in humans following animal experiments, immediately fail due to unexpected side effects or because they have no effect at all" (BWM 2020, p. 14; see also Mullard 2016). The call for alternative non-animal models is thus motivated by the double risk of (i) approving and prescribing drugs that are effective in standardized animals models, but that do not necessarily benefit the individual patient and may give a false sense of safety from adverse effects, and (ii) dismissing approval of drugs that could benefit individual patients, because they are not sufficiently effective in standardized animal models or average patients.[28] Clarifying how, and to what extent, cross-species inferences are possible – and whether there are better alternatives – are thus critically pressing issues.

The 3R principles have impacted regulations governing animal research in many countries. Yet, the replacement of animal models is developing slowly, and is according to Lohse (2021) hampered by "scientific inertia," understood as a certain degree of conservatism in science policy and scientific practice (see also Carusi, forthcoming). Lohse points out how barriers for adoption of NAMs include complex socio-epistemic factors such as existing regulatory standards, limited funding incentives, and lacking awareness of and training in non-animal approaches. The latter is also related to educational practices focused on animal models and the stabilizing role of animal models in research communities as central part of scientific repositories (see Ankeny and Leonelli 2016). Marshall and colleagues (2022) similarly observe that "in the European Union (and elsewhere), the overall use of animals in laboratories has failed to undergo any significant decline, despite six decades of purported adherence to the "3Rs" principles" (p. 1). But important changes may be about to happen. As mentioned in the introduction, the European Parliament has adopted an action plan to phase out animal testing, and a new law in the US allows for drug approval based on advanced in vitro models (Mullin 2023). We therefore next explore the promises of new alternative methods to complement or replace animal models.

6.3 Replacing Animal Models

Animal models have traditionally been considered superior to in vitro models as sources of translational evidence. This may change with NAMs, such as computer simulations and advanced in vitro methods such as organoids (Carusi, forthcoming). I briefly introduce the latter as an exciting topic for future philosophical work.

As the term "organoid" indicates, organoids are considered "organ-like" because they retain relevant features of the histology or the origin tissue. Organoids are cell cultures which are grown in a 3D basement membrane medium mimicking the physiological and biomechanical structures found in the body, including the composition of the extracellular matrix. Organoids can be based on cells derived from various sources, including embryonic stem cells, induced pluripotent stem cells (iPSCs), or adult (cancer) stem cells. The use of 3D

---

[28] It is important to note that animal models can improve translational research in other ways, e.g., by generating hypotheses about mechanisms underlying disease and treatment response (LaFollette and Shanks 1995; Leenaars et al. 2019). Yet, the translational failures do motivate rethinking of animal models as gold standards for evaluating drug efficacy and drug safety (Swaters et al. 2022).

cell cultures in biomedical research has a long history, particularly in cancer research and developmental biology (for a historical review, see Simian and Bissel 2017). But organoids have gained renewed attention following successful development of long-term 3D cultures capable of developing into miniature tissue structures. This was documented in two important publications in *Nature* showing how organoids derived from intestinal stem cells in mice and humans could self-organize into crypt-like structures resembling the tissues of in vivo intestines (Sato et al. 2009; Jung et al. 2011). Organoids have since been developed to mimic a variety of different tissue types, such as liver, brain, kidney, pancreas, lung, heart, the retina, as well as different diseases (e.g., tumors).

Compared to animal models, human organoids have the translational benefit of being developed directly from human cells, thus avoiding some of the translational gaps that result from species-specific differences. Patient-derived organoids are also promoted as promising tools for drug development and drug screening in precision medicine, because they can better represent the biological variation between patients (Bose et al. 2021). Moreover, organoids provide new opportunities for cell therapies and tissue engineering in regenerative medicine, which might address some of the epistemic and ethical challenges associated with traditional organ transplantation and chimeras in xenotransplantation (Vermeulen et al. 2017; Morata Tarifa et al. 2020). Rather than making animal models more like humans, the strategy is here to construct human-derived cell cultures resembling the in vivo tissue or organs. In a book on stem cell research, Thompson nicely frames the development of advanced culture models as a shift from "humanizing the animal model to *in-vivo*-izing the *in vitro* model" (Thompson 2013, p. 218).

Experimenting directly on the advanced cell cultures or simplified "mini-organs" of the sick human seems like a straightforward way to replace animals in translational research. Indeed, researchers in the field view organoids as being "as close to human in vivo as we can come" (interview quote in Hinterberger and Bea 2023, p. 3). Yet, Hinterberger and Bea also stress that the capacity of organoids to "model humanness" is enacted rather than given, and that using organoids to close translational gaps "requires constant scrutiny and validation" (p. 6). The scientific literature also states numerous challenges and limitations, with uncertainties revolving around the extent to which all relevant aspects of complex human diseases can be recapitulated "in a dish." But organoids are already becoming important tools for preclinical research because they can bridge some of the existing gaps between in vitro human models and in vivo animal models. Scientific reviews also point to benefits of organoids, compared to animal models, when studying molecular disease mechanisms and identifying potential treatment targets (Kim et al. 2020).

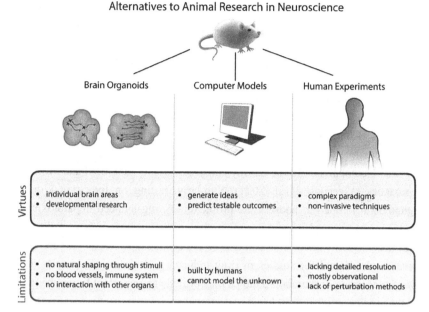

Figure 3 Virtues and limitations of animal-free methods in neuroscience, compared to rodent models. Reprinted from Homberg et al. (2021), with permission from Elsevier.

The prospect of *replacing* animal models with organoids is, however, an open question and currently field specific. Starting with one of the most challenging fields, behavioral neuroscience, an article written by 74 authors (Homberg et al. 2021) express concerns about unwarranted optimism about replacing animals in near future. Their view on the limitations of animal-free alternatives is illustrated in Figure 3. According to Homberg and colleagues, brain organoids provide exciting new models for intervening on neurological mechanisms in a simple system, but they currently have severe shortcomings in lacking vasculature or neural connections that link the brain structures to other organs or the immune system. Similarly, although the authors find computer simulations promising for generating and testing mechanistic hypotheses, they stress that *in silico* models are currently not able to push the field of behavioral neuroscience beyond what is currently known without data inputs from animal (or human) experimentation. While human experiments can provide many relevant data, these are typically non-invasive and mostly observational for ethical reasons. According to the authors, there are not yet any viable alternatives to animal experimentation in this field, and regulatory actions to replace animal models would be premature.

The outlined limitations of NAMs in behavioral science do, however, not diminish the potentials of and need for alternative models in other fields. For example, animal models are too resource-demanding to meet the increasing need for toxicity data for safety regulation of chemical compounds in consumer and agricultural products, industry, and medicine (Carusi et al. 2022a; 2022b). Computer simulations have also in some cases shown promising results in predicting the risk adverse effects of treatments, as exemplified by *in silico* drug trials demonstrating higher accuracy than animal models in predicting drug-induced cardiac arrhythmia (Passini et al. 2017), which calls for more systematic comparison of the validity and predictability of animal and *in silico* approaches (Viceconti et al. 2021). Similarly, testing on liver and kidney organoids are hoped to address the problems of drug-induced hepatotoxicity and kidney injuries, which remain among the major reasons for drug withdrawal from the market (Matsui and Shinozawa 2021). Intestinal organoids are also currently developed for studies of drug-induced gastrointestinal toxicity and allergic reactions, and brain organoids may provide an important future frontier for the prediction of drug-induced neurotoxicity.

Compared to in vivo animal models, organoids are very simple models. But it will be exciting to follow the development of advanced in vitro systems in the near future. For example, the limitation of the lacking vasculature is attempted to be addressed through development of so-called organ-on-chip (OoC) models. OoCs are microfluidic chips that connect human cells in a simplified vascular flow system on a plastic chip consisting of microchannels. These high-tech models are also hoped to provide higher control of experimental parameters and have showed promising results in toxicology tests based on liver cells (Ewart et al. 2022). But OoC models are still at an early stage of development and more evidence is needed to estimate if they are sufficiently predictive (Foo et al. 2022). Yet, even if animal models cannot be replaced by in vitro or in silico models, a combined approach using animal and non-animal methods can potentially help to prioritize (and thus reduce) the number of animals used in biomedical research. Moreover, NAMs as a growing research field may also fundamentally change evidence standards in translational research.

6.4 Toward New Evidence Standards in Translational Research?

Evidence-based medicine (EBM) traditionally emphasizes statistical power of large numbers and a high degree of standardization. Drawing again on Rosenblueth and Wiener's quote (1945), the slogan of the evidence hierarchy in EBM might be conceptualized as "the best model for a cat is as many similar cats as possible." The metaphor of "cats" here refers both to uniform animal models in preclinical trials and patient populations in clinical trials. But persistent translational challenges have spurred debates about the current evidence standards.

Advanced in vitro and *in silico* models may, however, alter evidence standards in medicine: away from standardized preclinical models and large clinical trials, towards models that are hoped to better capture patient variation. A precursor of this development may be seen in the use of organoid assays to screen for treatment efficacy in cases of rare disease, or rare disease subtypes (Bose et al. 2022). One such disease is cystic fibrosis (CF), where a so-called "swelling assay" can be used to screen for the efficacy of drugs targeting specific mutations. CF is caused by one or more mutations in the CF transmembrane conductance regulator (CFTR) gene, which causes disruptions in the proteins involved in transportation of chloride ions and water across cell membranes, often leading to thick mucus building up in the lungs. Despite being considered as a monocausal disease (caused by a dysfunction in the CFTR gene), CF is estimated to be caused by as many as 2000 different mutations which can influence the response to available treatments, including new (and expensive) CFTR modulating drugs (Kim et al. 2020). This provides a structural problem for drug approval, as standardized animal models are of limited use and there are often too few patients with specific mutations to make clinical trials possible. The so-called Forskolin Induces Swelling (FIS) assay was introduced in 2013, based on the observable differences in responses of intestinal cells of healthy people and CF patients to the drug Forskolin (Dekkers et al. 2016). The poorer the CFTR proteins function, the less swelling is observed in organoids. Combining Forskolin and CFTR-modulating drugs in a swelling assay of the CF patients' own cells can, however, help identify potentially beneficial treatments that work for the specific mutations of individual patients. The FIS swelling assay is therefore an interesting example of how NAMs may bridge existing translational gaps that can have important implications also for regulatory practices of drug approval and drug access (Mummery et al. 2021).

Similarly, in oncology, tumor organoids may be a promising way to account for the specific mutations of the individual patient's cancer cells. Compared to the "mouse avatars" discussed in Section 4.2, organoids are faster and less resource-demanding to develop. Tumor organoids from various cancer types have been developed and show promising predictive capacities when compared to both patients and animal models (Vlachogiannis et al. 2018; Kim et al. 2020; Bose et al. 2022). But there are also open questions about the ability to represent the complexity of in vivo human tumors with relatively simple organoid models in an artificial in vitro environment. Tumor organoids are grown in manufactured growth media, cultured from basement membrane extracts, typically from mouse sarcoma tumors (and are thus not completely animal-free), and they represent many relevant aspects of the typical tumor microenvironment.

Human in vitro models are also hoped to address the slow speed and high costs of drug development. It is not uncommon for translation from "bench to bedside" to take 10–15 years, with average investments of 1–6 billion US$ (Globe Newswire 2022). If precision medicine gains further traction, treatments will increasingly be developed for smaller patient groups. This requires rethinking of the current design of preclinical and clinical trials. Figure 4 illustrates the vision of speeding up the translational process and reducing both epistemic uncertainties and costs by letting human in vitro models substitute (many of) the current animals models in preclinical research. The figure also illustrates how the use of patient-derived organoids could potentially also reduce the number of patients needed in clinical trials, because there is less need for large clinical trials if in vitro models are superior in predicting the treatment response in individual patients or patient subgroups. Overall, the hope is thus that the use of advanced in vitro models could not only provide faster access to new treatments but also increase the predictability of preclinical and clinical models at the individual level.

Realization of the described vision crucially hinges on a demonstration of the predictive validity and clinical utility of the new in vitro models. For some diseases, particularly CF and cancer, organoids have been demonstrated to maintain relevant genetic and histological features of patient tissues and to predict treatment responses. Most of the existing evidences come from retrospective or parallel observational trials, so-called co-clinical trials, where the results of drug testing on organoids are compared to patient outcomes, and sometimes also to "competing" animal models (e.g., Dekkers et al. 2016; Vlachogiannis et al. 2018; Bose et al. 2022). These results give reasons for optimism concerning the potential of replacing some of the animal models currently used in preclinical studies, for both basic research and drug development. Whether the predictive capacity is also sufficiently robust to replace animals in drug safety testing and to guide treatment decisions in the clinic is still an open question, and evidence from interventional trials is still sparse and often inconclusive (e.g., Ooft et al. 2021). At present, the envisioned road to better and faster translation via altered evidence standards is currently paved with new uncertainties to be addressed in future studies, including the challenge to develop organoids fast enough for clinical decision-making in "real time," as discussed in Section 5.2 (Vogt et al. forthcoming).

Despite remaining uncertainties, organoids already facilitate access to experimental treatments for some patients with advanced and incurable cancer (Green et al. 2022). Similarly, organoid-based swelling assays are also used in

Drug discovery and approval

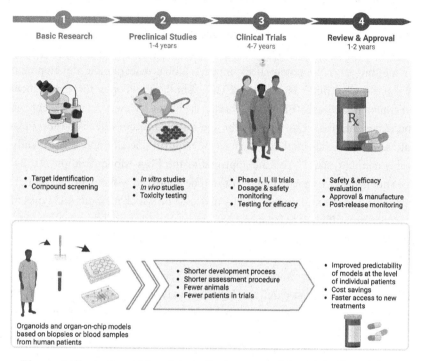

Figure 4 Illustration of the vision of using organoids and OoC models to improve the robustness and speed of translational research, inspired by a report by the Dutch Foundation for Biosciences and Society (2020, p. 12). The figure was created by the author with BioRender.com.

the Netherlands to guide treatment decisions for CF patients who have rare mutations that are not (yet) on the approved list for access to targeted treatments (Mummery et al. 2021, Chapter 10).[29] For patients with rare diseases or mutations, the evidence procedures suggested in Figure 4 can be a gamechanger, because the patient number is often too low to make large animal-based studies or human clinical trials economically and statistically feasible. Finally, some of the temporal challenges may be possible to address through so-called "living biobanks" containing cryopreserved organoids from patients with different mutational profiles. These are already being developed for some cancers as resources for preclinical research as well as for drug screening in cases where the individual patient's cancer cannot be established (fast enough) as organoids (Bose et al. 2021).

---

[29] This is based on the aforementioned "swelling assays" (Dekkers et al. 2016).

The approval of the FDA Modernization Act 2.0 has, not surprisingly, been met with enthusiasm from drug developers, biotech industry, and animal activist organizations. For example, Corbett, CEO of a company developing human-based chip technology argues that: "New alternative methods, such as Organ-on-a-Chip technology, are not only more predictive than animal model testing, but have the potential to improve global research and development productivity" (Globe Newswire 2022). Similarly, People for the Ethical Treatment of Animals (PETA) celebrates the bill as a victory on their webpage and states that the FDA will finally "be allowed to consider superior, non-animal drug testing methods, instead of requiring deadly and scientifically bogus animal tests."[30] Yet, the approval of the FDA Modernization Act 2.0 does not necessarily mean that drugs will be approved without animal models right away, as it is still up to the FDA to decide on which methods and types of evidence are sufficient to let specific drugs continue through the pipeline. And given the remaining uncertainties concerning the predictive validity of organoids in different contexts, it seems premature to conclude that the new alternative methods are superior in evaluating patient safety and drug efficacy. But we are entering an exciting phase that may greatly impact what will be considered the gold standard of translational research and safety regulation.

7 Wrapping up and Looking Ahead

This Element has explored different philosophical questions associated with human-directed animal models, understood as living organisms that are used in scientific research to study human disease. Philosophical attention to animal modeling is important not only for understanding how knowledge is produced in biomedical research but also how animal experimentation shapes our understanding of human diseases and our relationship with non-human species. Different translational models allow us to see different things and bring different theoretical perspectives – and ontologies – into being. Throughout the Element, I have tried to elucidate how persistent tensions between standardization and variation in medicine are negotiated and managed in practices of animal modeling and new alternative methods. Finally, animal modeling practices can also inform broader discussions about models in science, providing further illustration of the challenge of balancing the epistemic needs for reproduction and reduction of biological complexity.

---

[30] www.peta.org/action/action-alerts/victory-congress-passes-groundbreaking-fda-moderniza tion-act-2-0/?fbclid=IwAR1kKNoBqsDGgbOxWm6WfV_Cxe5WgYjWGjshX8062xOTiL-WMBE81h1H4DQ. Accessed December 30, 2023.

Specific animals are typically chosen as models because they share certain characteristics or physiological processes with humans and can therefore be used to study the underlying mechanisms of a particular condition or disease. However, model virtues in translational research are not reducible to representational similarity relations. Rather, the choice of animal models is highly dependent on contextual factors such as epistemic aims, ethical considerations, costs, available resources, as well as genetic or physiological features that make it possible to experimentally access a feature of interest or let animal models "stand in" for human patients. Some animals are even chosen because of the absence of human disease (negative models), and some serve more instrumental roles as diagnostic tools. We have also seen how model choices depend on options for engineering animal models for specific purposes and on the possibility of temporal alignment of model development with practical clinical purposes. Many of these issues need further philosophical exploration.

This Element has also hinted at intersections between discussions about animal models and how human diseases are perceived. We have for instance examined how standardization of mouse models and exploration of patient-derived models in cancer is intertwined with the emphasis on cancer as a genetic disease that is increasingly viewed as heterogenous. Similarly, the emphasis on "endophenotype models" in psychiatric research illustrates how model development in translational research does not always proceed from simple to more complex models. Rather, the focus on intermediate or endophenotype models is an attempt to bridge the gap between high-level complex disease and low-level causes, for example, by focusing on the impact of genetic variability on treatment response. For this purpose, the animal does not have to suffer from the same disease as the human counterpart but must display phenotypic traces that illustrate the effect of an intervention. In this process, the target does not always remain stable. Rather, epistemic uncertainties about translational models are intertwined with uncertainties about the nature of human diseases and shifting perspectives about what are the most salient features of these.

Capacities that unite humans and non-human animals are simultaneously paving the way for translational inferences and giving rise to ethical concerns and conflicts. The last section ended with a discussion of ongoing attempts to reduce and replace animal models, motivated in part by concerns about animal welfare but also by acknowledged limitations of animal models. These efforts include attempts to develop animal-free methods such as human in vitro models. About 15 years ago, Hunter (2008) pointed to the *paradox of model organisms*, that is, that the need for animal models "will only diminish once most of the fundamental mechanisms of biology have been solved to allow the greater use of both human tissue cultures and in silico methods for drug discovery. To reach that point, however, requires the extensive use of model organisms" (p. 719). Using organoids as models for basic research and phenotypic drug testing may speed up, or partly bypass, this process by providing complementary models that can better bridge the gap between two-dimensional cell culture models and animal studies. The emphasis on patient-derived preclinical and clinical models also reflects a possible shift in the drug development process, where orphan drugs are developed for increasingly smaller test populations, and patient-specific models are needed for individu-alized treatments and treatment testing. This raises fundamental philosophical questions about the possibility of representing human diseases "in a dish." Moreover, the attempt to replace animal models is not only confronted with epistemic uncertainties but also institutional and socio-epistemic barriers that will have to be addressed.

In summary, the use of animal models sheds light on the strategies pursued to both reduce and represent complexity, to measure and operationalize what is inaccessible in humans, and to address persistent tensions between standardiza-tion and variation in medicine. In a time where precision medicine is pushing for personalized models and treatment recommendations, debates about biomed-ical evidence keep swinging back to the question of whether and how know-ledge about individuals is dependent on *other lives* – animals as well as humans. We are facing a moment of potentially wide-ranging changes with new human in vitro models. Yet, uncertainties about animal models are not easily overcome by replacing them with animal-free methods, as they are intertwined with uncertainties also about the nature of human disease and what evidence is needed for robust decision-making in medicine.

References

Alder, M., & Easton, G. (2005). Human and veterinary medicine. *British Medical Journal, 330*(7496), 858–859.

Allen, T. M., Brehm, M. A., Bridges, S. et al.(2019). Humanized immune system mouse models: Progress, challenges and opportunities. *Nature Immunology, 20*(7), 770–774.

Ankeny, R. A. (2001). Model organisms as models: Understanding the "lingua franca" of the human genome project. *Philosophy of Science, 68*(S3), S251–S261.

Ankeny, R. A. (2007). Wormy logic: Model organisms as case-based reasoning. In A. N. H. Creager, E. Lunbeck, & M. N. Wise (Eds.), *Science without laws: Model systems, cases, exemplary narratives* (pp. 46–58). Durham, NC: Duke University Press.

Ankeny, R. A., & Leonelli, S. (2011). What's so special about model organisms? *Studies in History and Philosophy of Science Part A, 42*(2), 313–323.

Ankeny, R. A., & Leonelli, S. (2016). Repertoires: A post-Kuhnian perspective on scientific change and collaborative research. *Studies in History and Philosophy of Science, 60*, 18–28.

Ankeny, R. A., & Leonelli, S. (2020). *Model organisms.* Elements in the Philosophy of Biology. Cambridge: Cambridge University Press.

Ankeny, R. A., Leonelli, S., Nelson, N. C., & Ramsden, E. (2014). Making organisms model human behavior: Situated models in North-American alcohol research, since 1950. *Science in Context, 27*(3), 485–509.

Ankley, G. T., Bennett, R. S., Erickson, R. J. et al. (2010). Adverse outcome pathways: A conceptual framework to support ecotoxicology research and risk assessment. *Environmental Toxicology and Chemistry: An International Journal, 29*(3), 730–741.

Arluke, A., & Sanders, C. (1996). *Regarding Animals.* Philadelphia, PA: Temple University Press.

Baetu, T. M. (2014). Models and the mosaic of scientific knowledge: The case of immunology. *Studies in History and Philosophy of Biological and Biomedical Sciences, 45*, 49–56.

Baetu, T. M. (2016). The "big picture": The problem of extrapolation in basic research. *The British Journal for the Philosophy of Science, 67*, 941–964.

Bahr, J. M. (2008). The chicken as a model organism. In M. P. Conn (Ed.), *Sourcebook of models for biomedical research* (pp. 161–167). Totawa, NJ: Humana Press.

Bangi, E., Ang, C., Smibert, P. et al. (2019). A personalized platform identifies trametinib plus zoledronate for a patient with KRAS-mutant metastatic colorectal cancer. *Science Advances, 5*(5), eaav6528.

Barwich, A.-S. (2023). If Proust had whiskers: Recalling locations with smells. *Learning and Behavior, 51*, 121–122.

Batterman, R. W., & Rice, C. C. (2014). Minimal model explanations. *Philosophy of Science, 81*(3), 349–376.

Beacon, T. H., & Davie, J. R. (2021). The chicken model organism for epigenomic research. *Genome, 64*(4), 476–489.

Beery, A. K., & Kaufer, D. (2015). Stress, social behaviour, and resilience: Insights from rodents. *Neurobiology of Stress, 1*, 116–127.

Ben-David, U., Ha, G., Tseng, Y. Y. et al. (2017). Patient-derived xenografts undergo mouse-specific tumor evolution. *Nature genetics, 49*(11), 1567–1575.

Bix, G. J., Fraser, J. F., Mack, W. J. et al. (2018). Uncovering the Rosetta stone: Report from the first annual conference on key elements in translating stroke therapeutics from pre-clinical to clinical. *Translational Stroke Research, 9*, 258–266.

Bjernemose, M. S. Zebrafisk kan hjælpe med at lappe ødelagte menneskerter. Videnskab.dk, January 31, 2023, https://videnskab.dk/naturvidenskab/zebra fisk-kan-hjaelpe-med-at-lappe-oedelagte-menneskehjerter/.

Blum, M., & Ott, T. (2019). Xenopus: An undervalued model organism to study and model human genetic disease. *Cells Tissues Organs, 205*(5–6), 303–313.

Bolker, J. A. (2009). Exemplary and surrogate models: Two modes of representation in biology. *Perspectives in Biology and Medicine, 52*(4), 485–499.

Bolker, J. A. (2012). There's more to life than rats and flies. *Nature Comment, 491*, 31–33.

Bolker, J. A. (2017). Animal models in translational research: Rosetta stone or stumbling block? *Bioessays, 39*(12), 1700089.

Bolker, J. A., & Raff, R. A. (1997). Beyond worms, flies and mice: It's time to widen the scope of developmental biology. *Journal of NIH Research, 9*, 35–39.

Borges, J. L. (1954/1971). *A universal history of infamy* (N. T. di Giovanni, Trans., p. 131). Middlesex, UK: Penguin Books.

Bose, S., Barroso, M., Chheda, M. G. et al. (2022). A path to translation: How 3D patient tumor avatars enable next generation precision oncology. *Cancer Cell, 40*(12), 1448–1453.

Bose, S., Clevers, H., & Shen, X. (2021). Promises and challenges of organoid-guided precision medicine. *Med, 2*(9), 1011–1026.

Bradfute, S. B. (2023). History and impact of the mouse-adapted Ebola virus model. *Antiviral Research, 210*, 105493.

Bschir, K. (2017). Risk, uncertainty, and precaution in science: The Threshold of the Toxicological Concern approach in food toxicology. *Science and Engineering Ethics, 23*(2), 489–508.

Buffenstein, R., Park, T., Hanes, M., & Artwohl, J. E. (2012). Naked mole rat. In M. A. Suckow, K. A. Stevens, & R. P. Wilson (Eds.), *The laboratory rabbit, guinea pig, hamster, and other rodents* (pp. 1055–1074). London, UK: Academic Press.

Burggren, W. W. (1999). Developmental physiology, animal models, and the August Krogh principle. *Zoology, 102*, 148–156.

Burggren, W. W., & Warburton, S. (2007). Amphibians as animal models for laboratory research in physiology. *ILAR Journal, 48*(3), 260–269.

Burian, R. M. (1993). How the choice of experimental organism matters: Epistemological reflections on an aspect of biological practice. *Journal of the History of Biology, 26*(2), 351–367.

Cagan, R. L., Zon, L. I., & White, R. M. (2019). Modeling cancer with flies and fish. *Developmental Cell, 49*(3), 317–324.

Caipa Garcia, A. L., Arlt, V. M., & Phillips, D. H. (2022). Organoids for toxicology and genetic toxicology: Applications with drugs and prospects for environmental carcinogenesis. *Mutagenesis, 37*(2), 143–154.

Cait, J., Cait, A., Scott, R. W., Winder, C. B., & Mason, G. J. (2022). Conventional laboratory housing increases morbidity and mortality in research rodents: Results of a meta-analysis. *BMC Biology, 20*(1), 1–22.

Cambau, E., & Poljak, M. (2020). Sniffing animals as a diagnostic tool in infectious diseases. *Clinical Microbiology and Infection, 26*(4), 431–435.

Cao, Y., Vacanti, J. P., Paige, K. T., Upton, J., & Vacanti, C. A. (1997). Transplantation of chondrocytes utilizing a polymer-cell construct to produce tissue-engineered cartilage in the shape of a human ear. *Plastic and Reconstructive Surgery, 100*(2), 297–302.

Carbone, L. (2021). Estimating mouse and rat use in American laboratories by extrapolation from Animal Welfare Act-regulated species. *Scientific Reports, 11*(1), 493, 1–6.

Carusi, A. (forthcoming). Chemicals regulation and non-animal methods: Displacing the gold standard. *Wellcome Open Science.*

Carusi, A., Sanchez Dorado, J., & Sözüdogru, E. (2022a). *Adverse outcome pathway – Study report.* In C. Wittwehr & M. Whelan (Eds.), EUR 30925 EN (pp. 1–41). Luxembourg: Publication Office of the European Union.

Carusi, A., Wittwehr, C., & Whelan, M. (2022b). *Addressing evidence needs in chemicals policy and regulation.* EUR 30941 EN. Luxembourg: Publication Office of the European Union.

CBS News. (2020). Experts warn: Horseshoe crabs, crucial to helping create vaccines, are facing extinction. New York, November 9, 2020. www .cbsnews.com/newyork/news/horseshoe-crabs-vaccines-extinction/.

Changeux, J. P. (2006). The molecular biology of consciousness investigated with genetically modified mice. *Philosophical Transactions of the Royal Society B: Biological Sciences, 361,* 2239–2259.

Choutka, C., Cabrera, C., & Hirabayashi, S. (2022). Embracing complexity in Drosophila cancer models. *Disease Models & Mechanisms, 15*(3), dmm049513.

Connolly, K. A., Fitzgerald, B., Damo, M., & Joshi, N. S. (2022). Novel mouse models for cancer immunology. *Annual Review of Cancer Biology, 6,* 269–291.

Cronbach, L. J., & Meehl, P. E. (1955). Construct validity in psychological tests. *Psychological Bulletin, 52*(4), 281, 174–203.

Dam, M. S., Juhl, S. M., Sangild, P. T., & Svendsen, M. N. (2017). Feeding premature neonates: Kinship and species in translational neonatology. *Social Science & Medicine, 179,* 129–136.

Dam, M. S., Sangild, P. T., & Svendsen, M. N. (2018). Translational neonatology research: Transformative encounters across species and disciplines. *History and Philosophy of the Life Sciences, 40,* 1–16.

Dam, M. S., Sangild, P. T., & Svendsen, M. N. (2020). Plastic pigs and public secrets in translational neonatology in Denmark. *Palgrave Communications, 6*(1), 1–10.

Dam, M. S., & Svendsen, M. N. (2018). Treating pigs: Balancing standardisation and individual treatments in translational neonatology research. *BioSocieties, 13,* 349–367.

Davies, G. (2010). Captivating behavior: Mouse models, experimental genetics and reductionist returns in the neurosciences. *The Sociological Review, 58,* 53–72.

Davies, G. (2012). What is a humanized mouse? Remaking the species and spaces of translational medicine. *Body & Society, 18*(3–4), 126–155.

Davies, G. F., Greenhough, B. J., Hobson-West, P. et al. (2016). Developing a collaborative agenda for humanities and social scientific research on laboratory animal science and welfare. *PLoS One, 11*(7), e0158791.

Dekkers, J. F., Berkers, G., Kruisselbrink, E. et al. (2016). Characterizing responses to CFTR-modulating drugs using rectal organoids derived from subjects with cystic fibrosis. *Science Translational Medicine, 8*(344), 344ra84–344ra84.

De La Rochere, P., Guil-Luna, S., Decaudin, D. et al. (2018). Humanized mice for the study of immuno-oncology. *Trends in Immunology, 39*(9), 748–763.

Denayer, T., Stöhr, T., & Van Roy, M. (2014). Animal models in translational medicine: Validation and prediction. *New Horizons in Translational Medicine*, *2*(1), 5–11.

Dietrich, M. R., Ankeny, R. A., & Chen, P. M. (2014). Publication trends in model organism research. *Genetics*, *198*(3), 787–794.

Dietrich, M. R., Ankeny, R. A., Crowe, N., Green, S., & Leonelli, S. (2020). How to choose your research organism. *Studies in History and Philosophy of Science Part C: Studies in History and Philosophy of Biological and Biomedical Sciences*, *80*, 101227.

Dolberg, D. S., & Bissell, M. J. (1984). Inability of Rous sarcoma virus to cause sarcomas in the avian embryo. *Nature*, *309*(5968), 552–556.

Dutch Foundation for Biosciences and Society. (2020). *Mini Organs-on-Chips: Towards New Research Models for Studying Disease and Finding Treatments*. Dutch Foundation BMW, 3, 39, November 2020.

Efstathiou, S. (2019). Facing animal research. Levinas and technologies of effacement. In P. Peter Atterton & T. Wright (Eds.), *Face to face with animals. Levinas and the animal question* (pp. 139–164). Albany, NY: SUNY Press.

Ellenbroek, B., & Youn, J. (2016). Rodent models in neuroscience research: Is it a rat race? *Disease Models & Mechanisms*, *9*(10), 1079–1087.

Ellman, D. G., Slaiman, I. M., Mathiesen, S. B., Andersen, K. S., Hofmeister, W., Ober, E. A., & Andersen, D. C. (2021). Apex resection in zebrafish (Danio rerio) as a model of heart regeneration: A video-assisted guide. *International Journal of Molecular Sciences*, *22*(11), 5865.

Erick Peirson, B. R., Kropp, H., Damerow, J., & Laubichler, M. D. (2017). The diversity of experimental organisms in biomedical research may be influenced by biomedical funding. *BioEssays*, *39*(5), 1600258.

Ericsson, A. C., Crim, M. J., & Franklin, C. L. (2013). A brief history of animal modeling. *Missouri Medicine*, *110*(3), 201.

Ewart, L., Apostolou, A., Briggs, S. A. et al. (2022). Performance assessment and economic analysis of a human Liver-Chip for predictive toxicology. *Communications Medicine*, *2*(1), 154, 1–16.

Fazio, M., Ablain, J., Chuan, Y., Langenau, D. M., & Zon, L. I. (2020). Zebrafish patient avatars in cancer biology and precision cancer therapy. *Nature Reviews Cancer*, *20*(5), 263–273.

Foo, M. A., You, M., Chan, S. L. et al. (2022). Clinical translation of patient-derived tumour organoids-bottlenecks and strategies. *Biomarker Research*, *10*(1), 1–18.

Friese, C. (2013). Realising the potential of translational medicine: The uncanny emergence of care as science. *Current Anthropology*, *54*, S129–S138.

Friese, C., & Clarke, A. E. (2012). Transposing bodies of knowledge and technique: Animal models at work in reproductive sciences. *Social Studies of Science, 42*(1), 31–52.

Friese, C., Nuyts, N., & Pardo-Guerra, J. P. (2019). Cultures of care? Animals and science in Britain. *The British Journal of Sociology, 70*(5), 2042–2069.

Frommlet, F., & Heinze, G. (2021). Experimental replications in animal trials. *Laboratory Animals, 55*(1), 65–75.

García-Sancho, M., & Lowe, J. (2023). *A history of genomics across species, communities and projects.* Cham: Palgrave Macmillan.

Genzel, L. (2021). How to control behavioral studies for rodents – Don't project human thoughts onto them. *eNeuro 8*(1): ENEURO.0456–0420.2021.

Germain, P.-L. (2014). From replica to instruments: Animal models in biomedical research. *History and Philosophy of the Life Sciences, 36*(1), 114–128.

Globe Newswire. (2022). Congress approved landmark measure to reduce animal testing. Washington, DC. December 23. www.globenewswire.com/news-release/2022/12/23/2579295/0/en/Congress-Approves-Landmark-Measure-to-Reduce-Animal-Testing.html.

Godfrey-Smith, P. (2020). Varieties of subjectivity. *Philosophy of Science, 87*(5), 1150–1159.

Gorbunova, V., Takasugi, M., & Seluanov, A. (2020). Hyaluronan goes to great length. *Cell Stress, 4*(9), 227–229.

Grainger, R. M. (2012). *Xenopus tropicalis* as a model organism for genetics and genomics: Past, present, and future. *Xenopus Protocols: Post-Genomic Approaches, 917*, 3–15.

Green, S. (2013). When one model is not enough: Combining epistemic tools in systems biology. *Studies in History and Philosophy of Science Part C: Studies in History and Philosophy of Biological and Biomedical Sciences, 44*, 170–180.

Green, S. (2021). Cancer beyond genetics: On the practical implications of downward causation. In D. S. Brooks, J. DiFrisco, & W. C. Wimsatt (Eds.), *Levels of organization in the biological sciences* (pp. 195–213). Cambridge, MA: MIT Press.

Green, S., Dam, M. S., & Svendsen, M. N. (2021). Mouse avatars of human cancers: The temporality of translation in precision oncology. *History and Philosophy of the Life Sciences, 43*(1), 1–22.

Green, S., Dam, M. S., & Svendsen, M. N. (2022). Patient-derived organoids in precision oncology precision oncology–Towards a science of and for the individual? In C. Beneduce & M. Bertolaso (Eds.), *Personalized medicine in the making: Philosophical perspectives from biology to healthcare* (pp. 125–146). Cham: Springer International.

Green, S., Dietrich, M. R., Leonelli, S., & Ankeny, R. A. (2018). "Extreme" organisms and the problem of generalization: Interpreting the Krogh principle. *History and Philosophy of the Life Sciences, 40*(4), 1–22.

Gruen, L. (2003/2017). The moral status of animals. *Stanford Encyclopaedia of Philosophy.* https://plato.stanford.edu/entries/moral-animal/.

Guttinger, S., & Love, A. C. (2019). Characterizing scientific failure. Putting the replication crisis in context. *EMBO Reports, 20*, e48765.

Hanahan, D., Wagner, E. F., & Palmiter, R. D. (2007). The origins of oncomice: A history of the first transgenic mice genetically engineered to develop cancer. *Genes & Development, 21*(18), 2258–2270.

Hardesty, R. A. (2018). Much ado about mice: Standard-setting in model organism research. *Studies in History and Philosophy of Science Part C: Studies in History and Philosophy of Biological and Biomedical Sciences, 68*, 15–24.

Harding, J. D. (2017). Nonhuman primates and translational research: Progress, opportunities, and challenges. *ILAR Journal, 58*(2), 141–150.

Hau, H. (2008). Animal models for human diseases: An overview. In M. P. Conn (Ed.), *Sourcebook of models for biomedical research* (pp. 3–8). Totawa, NJ: Humana Press.

Hinterberger, A., & Bea, S. (2023). How do scientists model humanness? A qualitative study of human organoids in biomedical research. *Social Science & Medicine, 320*, 115676.

Homberg, J. R., Adan, R. A., Alenina, N. et al. (2021). The continued need for animals to advance brain research. *Neuron, 109*(15), 2374–2379.

Horowitz, B. N., Baccouche, B., Shivkumar, T. et al. (2020). The giraffe as a natural animal model for resistance to heart failure with preserved ejection fraction. *Preprints.org*, 1–13.

Huber, L., & Keuck, L. K. (2013). Mutant mice: Experimental organisms as materialised models in biomedicine. *Studies in History and Philosophy of Science Part C: Studies in History and Philosophy of Biological and Biomedical Sciences, 44*(3), 385–391.

Hunter, P. (2008). The paradox of model organisms. *EMBO Reports, 9*, 717–720.

Izumchenko, E., Paz, K., Ciznadija, D., Sloma, I., Katz, A., Vasquez-Dunddel, D., & Maki, R. (2017).Patient-derived xenografts effectively capture responses to oncology therapy in a heterogeneous cohort of patients with solid tumors. *Annals of Oncology, 28*(10), 2595–2605.

Jensen, A. M. B., & Svendsen, M. N. (2020). Collaborative intimacies: How research pigs in Danish organ transplantation facilitate medical training, moral reflection, and social networking. *Medicine Anthopology Theory, 7*(2), 120–149.

Jespersen, H., Lindberg, M. F., Donia, M. et al. (2017). Clinical responses to adoptive T-cell transfer can be modeled in an autologous immune-humanized mouse model. *Nature Communications, 8*(1), 1–10.

Jones, A. M., Chory, J., Dangl, J. L. et al. (2008). The impact of Arabidopsis on human health: Diversifying our portfolio. *Cell, 133*(6), 939–943.

Jones, R. C. (2022). Animal cognition and moral status. In B. Hale, A. Light, & L. Lawhon (Eds.), *The Routledge Companion to Environmental Ethics* (pp. 5–19). New York: Routledge.

Jung, P., Sato, T., Merlos-Suárez, A. et al. (2011). Isolation and in vitro expansion of human colonic stem cells. *Nature Medicine, 17*(10), 1225–1227.

Kalscheuer, H., Danzl, N., Onoe, T., et al. (2012). A model for personalized in vivo analysis of human immune responsiveness. *Science Translational Medicine, 4*(125), 125ra30–125ra30.

Keele, B. F., Jones, J. H., Terio, K. A. et al. (2009). Increased mortality and AIDS-like immunopathology in wild chimpanzees infected with SIVcpz. *Nature, 460*(7254), 515–519.

Kendler, K. S., & Neale, M. C. (2010). Endophenotype: A conceptual analysis. *Molecular Psychiatry, 15*(8), 789–797.

Key, B. (2015). Fish do not feel pain and its implications for understanding phenomenal consciousness. *Biology & Philosophy, 30*, 149–165.

Key, B. (2016). Why fish do not feel pain. *Animal Sentience, 1*(3), 1–33.

Kiani, A. K., Pheby, D., Henehan, G. et al. (2022). Ethical considerations regarding animal experimentation. *Journal of Preventive Medicine and Hygiene, 63*(2–3), E255–E266.

Kim, J., Koo, B. K., & Knoblich, J. A. (2020). Human organoids: Model systems for human biology and medicine. *Nature Reviews Molecular Cell Biology, 21*(10), 571–584.

Kirk, R. G. (2014). The invention of the "stressed animal" and the development of science of animal welfare, 1947–86. In D. Cantor & E. Ramadan (Eds.), *Stress, shock and adaptation in the twentieth century* (pp. 241–263). Rochester, NY: University of Rochester Press.

Kirk, R. G. (2018). Recovering the principles of humane experimental technique: The 3Rs and the human essence of animal research. *Science, Technology, & Human Values, 43*(4), 622–648.

Kirk, R. G., & Ramsden, E. (2018). Working across species down on the farm: Howard S. Liddell and the development of comparative psychopathology, c. 1923–1962. *History and Philosophy of the Life Sciences, 40*, 1–29.

Kleiber M. (1932). Body size and metabolism. *Hilgardia, 6*, 315–353.

Knuuttila, T. (2021). Epistemic artifacts and the modal dimension of modeling. *European Journal for Philosophy of Science, 11*(3), 1–18.

Kohler, R. E. (1994). *Lords of the fly: Drosophila and the experimental life.* Chicago, IL: University of Chicago Press.

Krebs, H. A. (1975). The August Krogh Principle: "For many problems there is an animal on which it can be most conveniently studied". *Journal of Experimental Zoology, 194,* 221–226.

Krisfalusi-Gannon, J., Ali, W., Dellinger, K. et al. (2018). The role of horseshoe crabs in the biomedical industry and recent trends impacting species sustainability. *Frontiers in Marine Science, 5,* 1–13.

Krogh, A. (1910). On the mechanism of the gas-exchange in the lungs of the tortoise. *Skandinavisches Archiv für Physiologie, 23*(1), 200–216.

Krogh, A. (1929). Progress in physiology. *American Journal of Physiology, 90,* 243–251.

LaFollette, H., & Shanks, N. (1993). Animal models in biomedical research: Some epistemological worries. *Public Affairs Quarterly, 7*(2), 113–130.

LaFollette, H., & Shanks, N. (1995). Two models of models in biomedical research. *The Philosophical Quarterly, 45*(179), 141–160.

Larsen, E. H., Hoffmann, E., Hedrick, M. S., & Wang, T. (2021). August Krogh's contribution to the rise of physiology during the first half the 20th century. *Comparative Biochemistry and Physiology Part A: Molecular & Integrative Physiology, 256,* 110931.

Leavitt, Sarah A. (2006). "A private little revolution": The home pregnancy test in American culture. *Bulletin of the History of Medicine, 80,* 317–345.

Leenaars, C. H., Kouwenaar, C., Stafleu, F. R. et al. (2019). Animal to human translation: A systematic scoping review of reported concordance rates. *Journal of Translational Medicine, 17*(1), 1–22.

Lemoine, M. (2015). Extrapolation from animal model of depressive disorders: What's lost in translation? In J. C. Wakefield & S. Demazeux (Eds.), *Sadness or depression? International perspectives on the depression epidemic and its meaning* (pp. 157–172). Heidelberg, New York: Springer.

Leonelli, S. (2007). Growing weed, producing knowledge an epistemic history of Arabidopsis thaliana. *History and Philosophy of the Life Sciences, 29*(2), 193–223.

Leonelli, S. (2016). *Data-Centric Biology: A Philosophical Study.* Chicago, IL: University of Chicago Press.

Leonelli, S., & Ankeny, R. A. (2012). Re-thinking organisms: The impact of databases on model organism biology. *Studies in History and Philosophy of Science Part C: Studies in History and Philosophy of Biological and Biomedical Sciences, 43*(1), 29–36.

Levy, A., & Currie, A. (2015). Model organisms are not (theoretical) models. *The British Journal for the Philosophy of Science, 66,* 327–348.

Lewis, J., Atkinson, P., Harrington, J., & Featherstone, K. (2013). Representation and practical accomplishment in the laboratory: When is an animal model good-enough? *Sociology, 47*(4), 776–792.

Liddell, H. S. (1942). The alteration of instinctual processes through the influence of conditioned reflexes. *Psychosomatic Medicine, 4*, 390–395.

Lohse, S. (2021). Scientific inertia in animal-based research in biomedicine. *Studies in History and Philosophy of Science Part A, 89*, 41–51.

Logan, C. A. (2002). Before there were standards: The role of test animals in the production of scientific generality in physiology. *Journal of the History of Biology, 35*, 329–363.

Love, A. (2007). Functional homology and homology of function: Biological concepts and philosophical consequences. *Biology and Philosophy, 22*, 691–708.

Love, A. (2010). Idealization in evolutionary developmental investigation: A tension between phenotypic plasticity and normal stages. *Philosophical Transactions of the Royal Society B, 365*, 679–690.

Lowe, J., Leng, R., Viry, G. et al. (2022). The bricolage of pig genomics. *Historical Studies in the Natural Sciences, 52*(3), 401–442.

Lowe, J. W. (2022). Humanising and dehumanising pigs in genomic and transplantation research. *History and Philosophy of the Life Sciences, 44* (4), 1–27.

Lowe, J. W., Leonelli, S., & Davies, G. (2020). Training to translate: Understanding and informing translational animal research in pre-clinical pharmacology. *TECNOSCIENZA: Italian Journal of Science & Technology Studies, 10*(2), 5–30.

Lunney, J. K., Van Goor, A., Walker, K. E. et al. (2021). Importance of the pig as a human biomedical model. *Science Translational Medicine, 13*(621), eabd5758.

Malaney, P., Nicosia, S. V., & Davé, V. (2014). One mouse, one patient paradigm: New avatars of personalized cancer therapy. *Cancer Letters, 344*(1), 1–12.

Maloney, T., Phelan, R., & Simmons, N. (2018). Saving the horseshoe crab: A synthetic alternative to horseshoe crab blood for endotoxin detection. *PLoS Biology, 16*(10), e2006607.

Marcus, B. (2016). LSD and the elephant. *Illinois Science Council. Science Unsealed Blog*, June 27, 2016, www.illinoisscience.org/2016/06/lsd-and-the-elephant/.

Marshall, L. J., Constantino, H., & Seidle, T. (2022). Phase-in to phase-out – Targeted, inclusive strategies are needed to enable full replacement of animal use in the European Union. *Animals, 12*(7), 863.

Matsui, T., & Shinozawa, T. (2021). Human organoids for predictive toxicology research and drug development. *Frontiers in Genetics*, *1–18*, 2119. https://doi.org/10.3389/fgene.2021.767621.

Maugeri, P., & Blasimme, A. (2011). Humanised models of cancer in molecular medicine: The experimental control of disanalogy. *History and Philosophy of the Life Sciences*, *33*(4), 603–621.

Maxson Jones, K., & Morgan, J. R. (2023). Lampreys and spinal cord regeneration: "A very special claim on the interest of zoologists," 1830s-present. *Frontiers in Cell and Developmental Biology*, *11*, 1113961.

Mazarati, A. (2007). The best model for a cat is the same cat . . . or is it? *Epilepsy Currents*, *7*(4), 112–114.

Mian, S. A., Anjos-Afonso, F., & Bonnet, D. (2021). Advances in human immune system mouse models for studying human hematopoiesis and cancer immunotherapy. *Frontiers in Immunology*, *11*, 619236.

Mol, A., Moser, I., & Pols, J. (Eds.). (2010). *Care in practice: On tinkering in clinics, homes and farms*. Bielefeld: Transcript Verlag.

Morata Tarifa, C., López Navas, L., Azkona, G., & Sánchez Pernaute, R. (2020). Chimeras for the twenty-first century. *Critical Reviews in Biotechnology*, *40*(3), 283–291.

Morrison, M., & Morgan, M. (1999). Models as mediating instruments. In M. Morrison & M. S. Morgan (Eds.), *Models as mediators: Perspectives on natural and social science* (pp. 10–37). Cambridge, MA: Cambridge University Press.

Morthorst, J. E., Holbech, H., De Crozé, N., Matthiessen, P., & LeBlanc, G. A. (2023). Thyroid-like hormone signaling in invertebrates and its potential role in initial screening of thyroid hormone system disrupting chemicals. *Integrated Environmental Assessment and Management*, *19*(1), 63–82.

Mullard, A. (2016). Parsing clinical success rates. *Nature Reviews Drug Discovery*, *15*(7), 447–448.

Mullin, E. (2023). The US just greenlit high-tech alternatives to animal testing. *Wired*, January 11, 2023.

Mummery, C., Van de Stolpe, A., Roelen, B., & Clevers, H. (2021). *Stem cells: Scientific facts and fiction* (3rd ed.). London, UK: Academic Press.

Nair, A. B., & Jacob, S. (2016). A simple practice guide for dose conversion between animals and human. *Journal of Basic and Clinical Pharmacy*, *7*(2), 27–31.

Nelson, N. C. 2013. Modeling mouse, human, and discipline: Epistemic scaffolds in animal behavior genetics. *Social Studies of Science*, *43*(1), 3–29.

Nelson, N. C. 2018. *Model behavior: Animal experiments, complexity, and the genetics of psychiatric disorders*. Chicago, IL: University of Chicago Press.

Nilsson, J. A., Olofsson Bagge, R., & Ny, L. (2018). Mouse avatars take off as cancer models. *Nature, 562*(7726), 192–192.

Nissinen, J., & Pitkänen, A. (2007). Effect of antiepileptic drugs on spontaneous seizures in epileptic rats. *Epilepsy Research, 73*(2), 181–191.

Olszynko-Gryn, J. (2013). When pregnancy test were toads: The Xenopus test in the early NHS. *Wellcome History, 51*, 1–3.

Olszynko-Gryn, J. (2014). The demand for pregnancy testing: The Aschheim–Zondek reaction, diagnostic versatility, and laboratory services in 1930s Britain. *Studies in History and Philosophy of Science Part C: Studies in History and Philosophy of Biological and Biomedical Sciences, 47*, 233–247.

Ooft, S. N., Weeber, F., Schipper, L. et al. (2021). Prospective experimental treatment of colorectal cancer patients based on organoid drug responses. *ESMO Open, 6*(3), 100103.

Panksepp, J. (1998). *Affective neuroscience: The foundations of human and animal emotions*. Oxford: Oxford University Press.

Parkkinen, V.-P. (2017). Are model organisms theoretical models? *Disputatio, 9*, 471–498.

Passini, E., Britton, O. J., Lu, H. R. et al. (2017). Human in silico drug trials demonstrate higher accuracy than animal models in predicting clinical pro-arrhythmic cardiotoxicity. *Frontiers in Physiology, 8*, 1–15.

Perlman, R. L. (2016). Mouse models of human disease: An evolutionary perspective. *Evolution, Medicine, and Public Health, 1*, 170–176.

Perry, S. (2013). Mouse "avatars" advance personalized medicine. *Endocrine News*, January 2013. https://endocrinenews.endocrine.org/mouse-avatars-advance-personalized-medicine/

Piotrowska, M. (2013). From humanized mice to human disease: Guiding extrapolation from model to target. *Biology & Philosophy, 28*, 439–455.

Preson, E. (2022). Octopuses don't have backbones – or rights. *The New York Times*, August 27, 2022.

Rader, K. A. (2004). *Making mice. Standardizing animals for American biomedical research, 1900–1955*. Princeton, NJ: Princeton University Press.

Ramhøj, L., Axelstad, M., Baert, Y. et al. (2023). New approach methods to improve human health risk assessment of thyroid hormone system disruption – A PARC project. *Frontiers in Toxicology, 5*, 1189303.

Ramsden, E. (2015). Making animals alcoholic: Shifting laboratory models of addiction. *Journal of the History of the Behavioral Sciences, 51*(2), 164–194.

Ramsey, G. (2013). Culture in humans and other animals. *Biology & Philosophy, 28*, 457–479.

Ramsey, G. (2023). *Human Nature*. Elements in the Philosophy of Biology. Cambridge: Cambridge University Press.

Rankin, K. S., & Frankel, D. (2016). Hyaluronan in cancer – From the naked mole rat to nanoparticle therapy. *Soft Matter, 12*(17), 3841–3848.

Ransohoff, R. M. 2018. All (animal) models (of neurodegeneration) are wrong. Are they also useful? *The Journal of Experimental Medicine, 215*, 2955–2958.

Rasmussen, A. L., Okumura, A., Ferris, M. T. et al. (2014). Host genetic diversity enables Ebola hemorrhagic fever pathogenesis and resistance. *Science, 346*(6212), 987–991.

Ratti, E. (2020). "Models of" and "Models for": On the relation between mechanistic models and experimental strategies in molecular biology. *The British Journal for the Philosophy of Science, 71*, 773–797.

Reardon, S. (2022). First pig-to-human heart transplant: What can scientists learn? *Nature, 601*(7893), 305–306.

Regan, T. (1983). *The case for animal rights*. Berkeley, CA: University of California Press.

Rheinberger, H.-J. (1997). *Toward a History of Epistemic Things. Synthesising Proteins in the Test Tube*. Stanford CA: Stanford University Press.

Rosenblueth, A., & Wiener, N. (1945). The role of models in science. *Philosophy of Science, 12*(4), 316–321.

Russell, J. J., Theriot, J. A., Sood, P. et al. (2017). Non-model model organisms. *BMC Biology, 15*(1), 1–31.

Russell, W. M. S., & Burch, R. L. (1959). *The principles of humane experimental technique*. London UK: Methuen and Co Ltd.

Sangild, P. T., Thymann, T., Schmidt, M. et al. (2014). The preterm pig as a model in pediatric gastroenterology. *Journal of Animal Science, 91*(10), 4713–4729.

Sato, T., Vries, R. G., Snippert, H. J. et al. (2009). Single Lgr5 stem cells build crypt-villus structures in vitro without a mesenchymal niche. *Nature, 459* (7244), 262–265.

Schaffner, K. F. (1986). Exemplar reasoning about biological models and diseases: A relation between the philosophy of medicine and philosophy of science. *The Journal of Medicine and Philosophy, 11*, 63–80.

Schaffner, K. F. (2001). Extrapolation from animal models: Social life, sex, and super models. In P. K. Machamer, R. Grush, & P. McLaughlin (Eds.), *Theory and method in the neurosciences* (pp. 200–230). Pittsburgh, PA: University of Pittsburgh Press.

Schmidt-Nielsen, B. (1995/2019). *August & Marie Krogh: Lives in science*. Oxford, NY: American Physiological Society. Reprinted by the University of Copenhagen, Denmark.

Schmidt-Nielsen, K. (1984). *Scaling: Why is animal size so important?* Cambridge: Cambridge University Press.

Scudellari, M. (2015). My mighty mouse. *The Scientist*, March 31, 2015, www.thescientist.com/cover-story/my-mighty-mouse-35712

Shanks, N., Greek, R., & Greek, J. (2009). Are animal models predictive for humans? *Philosophy, Ethics, and Humanities in Medicine, 4*(1), 2.

Sharp, L. A. (2013). *The transplant imaginary: Mechanical hearts, animal parts, and moral thinking in highly experimental science.* Berkeley, CA: University of California Press.

Sharp, L. A. (2019). *Animal ethos: The morality of human-animal encounters in experimental lab science.* Oakland, CA: University of California Press.

Simian, M., & Bissell, M. J. (2017). Organoids: A historical perspective of thinking in three dimensions. *Journal of Cell Biology, 216*(1), 31–40.

Singer, P. (1975). *Animal liberation: A new ethics for our treatment of animals.* New York: HarperCollins.

Smith, J. A., Andrews, P. L., Hawkins, P. et al. (2013). Cephalopod research and EU Directive 2010/63/EU: Requirements, impacts and ethical review. *Journal of Experimental Marine Biology and Ecology, 447*, 31–45.

Smith, J. R., Hayman, G. T., Wang, S. J. et al. (2020). The year of the rat: The rat genome database at 20: A multi-species knowledgebase and analysis platform. *Nucleic Acids Research, 48*(D1), D731–D742.

Sneddon, L. U. (2015). Pain in aquatic animals. *The Journal of Experimental Biology, 218*(7), 967–976.

Sneddon, L. U., & Leach, M. C. (2016). Anthropomorphic denial of fish pain. *Animal Sentience, 3*(28), 1–3.

Star, S. L. (1983). Simplification in scientific work: An example from neuroscience research. *Social Studies of Science, 13*, 208–226.

Steel, D. (2008). *Across the boundaries: Extrapolation in biology and social science.* Oxford: Oxford University Press.

Stegenga, J. (2022). Evidence of effectiveness. *Studies in History and Philosophy of Science, 91*, 288–295.

Stegman, U. E. (2021). Medical toolkit organisms and Covid-19. *History and Philosophy of the Life Sciences, 43*, 14.

Stewart, T. A., Pattengale, P. K., & Leder, P. (1984). Spontaneous mammary adenocarcinomas in transgenic mice that carry and express MTV/*myc* fusion genes. *Cell, 38*, 627–637.

Stoker, A. W., Hatier, C., & Bissell, M. J. (1990). The embryonic environment strongly attenuates v-src Oncogenesis in mesenchymal and epithelial tissues, but not in endothelia. *Journal of Cell Biology, 111*(1), 217–228.

Striedter, G. F. (2022). *Model systems in biology. History, philosophy, and practical concerns.* Cambridge, MA: MIT Press.

Suntsova, M. V., & Buzdin, A. A. (2020). Differences between human and chimpanzee genomes and their implications in gene expression, protein functions and biochemical properties of the two species. *BMC Genomics, 21*(7), 1–12.

Svendsen, M. N. (2022). *Near human: Border zones of species, life, and belonging.* New Brunswick, Camden: Rutgers University Press.

Svendsen, M. N., & Koch, L. (2013). Potentializing the research piglet in experimental neonatal research. *Current Anthropology, 54*(S7), S118–S128.

Swaters, D., van Veen, A., van Meurs, W., Turner, J. E., & Ritskes-Hoitinga, M. (2022). A history of regulatory animal testing: What can we learn? *Alternatives to Laboratory Animals, 50*(5), 322–329.

Szpirer, C. (2020). Rat models of human diseases and related phenotypes: A systematic inventory of the causative genes. *Journal of Biomedical Science, 27*(1), 1–52.

Taylor, K., & Alvarez, L. R. (2019). An estimate of the number of animals used for scientific purposes worldwide in 2015. *Alternatives to Laboratory Animals, 47*(5–6), 196–213.

Thompson, C. (2013). *Good science: The ethical choreography of stem cell research.* Cambridge, MA: MIT Press.

Tian, X., Azpurua, J., Hine, C. et al. (2013). High-molecular-mass hyaluronan mediates the cancer resistance of the naked mole rat. *Nature, 499*(7458), 346–349.

Valenzano, D. R., Aboobaker, A., Seluanov, A., & Gorbunova, V. (2017). Non-canonical aging model systems and why we need them. *The EMBO Journal, 36*(8), 959–963.

van Akker, R., Balls, M., Eichberg, J. W. et al. (1994). Chimpanzees in AIDS research: A biomedical and bioethical perspective. *Journal of Medical Primatology, 23*, 49–51.

Veit, W. (2022). Towards a comparative study of animal consciousness. *Biological Theory, 17*, 292–303.

Venniro, M., Banks, M. L., Heilig, M., Epstein, D. H., & Shaham, Y. (2020). Improving translation of animal models of addiction and relapse by reverse translation. *Nature Reviews Neuroscience, 21*(11), 625–643.

Vermeulen, N., Haddow, G., Seymour, T., Faulkner-Jones, A., & Shu, W. (2017). 3D bioprint me: A socioethical view of bioprinting human organs and tissues. *Journal of Medical Ethics, 43*(9), 618–624.

Viceconti, M., Pappalardo, F., Rodriguez, B. et al. (2021). *In silico* trials: Verification, validation and uncertainty quantification of predictive models used in the regulatory evaluation of biomedical products. *Methods*, *185*, 120–127.

Vlachogiannis, G., Hedayat, S., Vatsiou, A. et al. (2018). Patient-derived organoids model treatment response of metastatic gastrointestinal cancers. *Science*, *359*(6378), 920–926.

Vogt, H., Maxence, G., & Green, S. (forthcoming). D2.4: An amended health technology assessment (HTA) to evaluate organoids as emerging technologies in the clinic. EU report (available soon online).

Wang, T. (2011). Gas exchange in frogs and turtles: How ectothermic vertebrates contributed to solving the controversy of pulmonary oxygen secretion. *Acta Physiologica*, *202*(3), 593–600.

Waters, C. K. (2008). How practical know-how contextualizes theoretical knowledge: Exporting causal knowledge from laboratory to nature. *Philosophy of Science*, *75*(5), 707–719.

Weber, M. (2001). Under the lamppost: Commentary on Schaffner. In P. Machamer, R. Grush, & P. McLaughlin (Eds.), *Theory and method in the neurosciences* (pp. 231–249). Pittsburgh, PA: University of Pittsburgh Press.

Weber, M. (2005). *Philosophy of experimental biology*. Cambridge: Cambridge University Press.

West, G. (2017). *Scale: The universal laws of growth, innovation, sustainability, and the pace of life in organisms, cities, economies, and companies*. New York: Penguin Press.

West, L. J., Pierce, C. M., & Thomas, W. D. (1962). Lysergic acid diethylamide: Its effects on a male Asiatic elephant. *Science*, *138*(3545), 1100–1103.

Willyard, C. (2018). The mice with human tumours: Growing pains for a popular cancer model. *Nature News Feature*, *560*(7717), 156.

Wittwehr, C., Aladjov, H., Ankley, G. et al. (2017). How adverse outcome pathways can aid the development and use of computational prediction models for regulatory toxicology. *Toxicological Sciences*, *155*(2), 326–336.

Woodward, J. (2003). *Making things happen: A theory of explanation*. New York: Oxford University Press.

Würbel, H. (2002). Behaviour and the standardization fallacy. *Nature Genetics*, *26*, 263.

Xu, C., Li, X., Liu, P., Li, M., & Luo, F. (2019). Patient-derived xenograft mouse models: A high fidelity tool for individualized medicine. *Oncology Letters*, *17*(1), 3–10.

Zanella, E. R., Grassi, E., & Trusolino, L. (2022). Towards precision oncology with patient-derived xenografts. *Nature Reviews Clinical Oncology*, *19*(11), 719–732.

Acknowledgements

I would like to thank Grant Ramsey for taking on the hard work of editing the Cambridge Element Series on philosophy of biology and for giving me the opportunity to contribute. My exploration of the epistemic and ethical dimensions of using animal models for human disease research is inspired by the work of and collaborations with esteemed colleagues, including Sabina Leonelli, Rachel Ankeny, Michael Dietrich, Mette Nordahl Svendsen, Mie Seest Dam, Lara Keuck, and many others. I express appreciation to Javier Suárez, Mette Nordahl Svendsen, Mie Seest Dam, Robert Batterman, and two anonymous reviewers for their valuable feedback on an earlier version of this Element. I also thank the production manager, Dhanalakshmi Narayanan, for help with copy-editing of the whole text.

Cambridge Elements ≡

Philosophy of Biology

Grant Ramsey

KU Leuven

Grant Ramsey is a BOFZAP research professor at the Institute of Philosophy, KU Leuven, Belgium. His work centers on philosophical problems at the foundation of evolutionary biology. He has been awarded the Popper Prize twice for his work in this area. He also publishes in the philosophy of animal behavior, human nature and the moral emotions. He runs the Ramsey Lab (theramseylab.org), a highly collaborative research group focused on issues in the philosophy of the life sciences.

Michael Ruse

Florida State University

Michael Ruse is the Lucyle T. Werkmeister Professor of Philosophy and the Director of the Program in the History and Philosophy of Science at Florida State University. He is Professor Emeritus at the University of Guelph, in Ontario, Canada. He is a former Guggenheim fellow and Gifford lecturer. He is the author or editor of over sixty books, most recently *Darwinism as Religion: What Literature Tells Us about Evolution*; *On Purpose*; *The Problem of War: Darwinism, Christianity, and their Battle to Understand Human Conflict*; and *A Meaning to Life*.

About the Series

This Cambridge Elements series provides concise and structured introductions to all of the central topics in the philosophy of biology. Contributors to the series are cutting-edge researchers who offer balanced, comprehensive coverage of multiple perspectives, while also developing new ideas and arguments from a unique viewpoint.

Cambridge Elements ☰

Philosophy of Biology

Printed in the United States
by Baker & Taylor Publisher Services